Mary Virginia Robinson
— November 1991.

SIERRA CLUB

100 YEARS
OF PROTECTING
NATURE

SIERRA CLUB

100 YEARS
OF PROTECTING
NATURE

BY TOM TURNER

PUBLISHED BY HARRY N. ABRAMS, INC.
IN ASSOCIATION WITH THE SIERRA CLUB

ANNE HOY
EDITOR

RAYMOND P. HOOPER
DESIGNER

NEIL RYDER HOOS
PHOTO RESEARCH

DIANA LANDAU
SIERRA CLUB CONSULTANT

Photographs credited in the captions to the Sierra Club Archives are located in the William E. Colby Library, Sierra Club, San Francisco, and the Bancroft Library, University of California, Berkeley.

All illustrations are from the Sierra Club Archives or files, were formerly reproduced in Sierra Club publications, or represent the work of photographers known through Sierra Club books. Exceptions are the images from the Oakland Museum in the foreword and chapter 1 and the photographs shown on pp. 192, 193 (top), and 222.

Given titles of works are capitalized in the captions; all other titles are descriptive.

Library of Congress Cataloging-in-Publication Data

Turner, Tom, 1942–
Sierra Club : 100 years of protecting nature / by Tom Turner :
introduction by Frederick Turner : foreword by Richard Leonard and
Susan Merrow.
p.   cm.
Includes bibliographical references (p. 282) and index.
ISBN 0-8109-3820-0
1. Sierra Club — History. 2. Nature conservation — United States —
History. I. Title.
QH76.T87   1991
333.9516′06073 — dc20   91-9866

Endpapers: *Carr Clifton* (front), The Chinese Wall, Bob Marshall Wilderness, Montana. 1989. (back) Banner Peak, Thousand Island Lake, Ansel Adams Wilderness, California. 1989

Opposite title page: *Larry Ulrich.* El Capitan, Yosemite Valley, Yosemite National Park, California. 1985

Opposite table of contents: *Ansel Adams.* El Capitan, Winter, Yosemite Valley National Park, California. 1948. © 1991 Trustees of the Ansel Adams Publishing Rights Trust

THIS BOOK
IS DEDICATED
TO THE MEMBERS
OF THE
SIERRA CLUB

CONTENTS

FOREWORD

One hundred years may be the blink of an eye in the history of our planet, but one hundred years of Sierra Club history have left an indelible mark for the better on planet earth. We are very proud of what we have accomplished in protecting the earth's wild places, its natural resources, and the environment on which all humankind depends. The story of this remarkable institution is best told not just in words but also in pictures that represent the beauty of the earth we are committed to protect and the tens of thousands of people from all walks of life, starting with John Muir, who have been the lifeblood of the Club and its successes.

John Muir knew that there is a fundamental, vital connectedness between nature and its creatures and humankind, and that we have a responsibility to work for their protection. This vision must have been at the center of Muir's thinking as he looked forward to the founding meeting of the Sierra Club, writing that he was "hoping to do something for wildness and make the mountains glad."

Since Muir's time, the Sierra Club has grown immensely. There are close to three-quarters of a million members, with active groups in every state and a number of Canadian provinces. Virtually every night of the year, there is at least one Sierra Club group, committee, or task force meeting in someone's living room — or by telephone conference call or even through computer dialogue. Sierra Club outings no longer focus on the Sierra Nevada alone but truly explore and enjoy the earth's wild places.

It is important that we celebrate and learn from our past because the future is about to call on our skills and resources with unprecedented urgency. The nature and complexity of environmental problems that concern the Sierra Club have grown as the world population has multiplied and become more technologically sophisticated. The issues are not simple, not readily reduced to good or bad. We do know, however, that we are affecting delicate global processes by pollution from our daily activities. The United States-Iraq war was based in part on exploitation of a natural resource; the conflict brought profound destruction to the region. Around the globe, plant and animal species, including their essential genetic information, and wilderness itself, where nature's richness is created, are disappearing at an alarming and accelerating rate.

Human activity has changed the atmosphere, the fragile bubble that surrounds our beautiful small planet and gives life to all that we hold dear — all that we have pledged to defend, enjoy, and protect. There is no priority more

8

urgent than bringing to reality Muir's vision of humanity living in harmony with the earth. It is this vision that continues to sustain us as the Sierra Club moves forward into its second century.

We envision a world where wilderness areas and open spaces are protected habitats sustaining all species—a world where oceans and streams are clean and the air is pure—a world where a healthy biosphere and a nontoxic environment are inalienable rights. In short, we envision a world saved from the threat of unalterable planetary disaster.

People must learn to live in ways that preserve and protect our irreplaceable resources. Our institutions must abandon practices that recklessly endanger the environment. Progress must be measured by its long-term value to living systems and creatures rather than its short-term value to special economic interests. People across the nation and around the world must speak out with a voice that cannot be ignored. Action on a global scale is essential to protect our environment and our species. There is no other choice.

These are daunting challenges, but as an organization we have always risen to challenges. We learned long ago that the best strategies only work when they are coupled with the individual actions of an ardent and dedicated community of activists. It is that community, surviving, growing, and becoming stronger, that we applaud in this book.

The essential ingredient of the Sierra Club's successes has been the commitment of extraordinary people: not only its activist volunteer leaders and staff but also its more than one million members over the years, who have participated in its activities, written letters, and supported it through their membership and additional financial contributions. Without them, the Sierra Club would be nothing. In celebration of their commitment, we dedicate this book to those who give us our strength: the members of the Sierra Club.

As the Club prepares for its second century, members and staff together offer America and the world our vision of humanity living in harmony with nature. We—each of us who make up the Sierra Club community—dedicate ourselves to achieving this vision as we reaffirm our passionate commitment to explore, enjoy, and protect the earth.

Richard Leonard
HONORARY PRESIDENT
Sierra Club

Susan Merrow
PRESIDENT
Sierra Club

INTRODUCTION

❧

THE
AMERICAN LAND
AND
THE HISTORY
OF HOPE

❧

Five hundred years after its invention by the European imagination, America keeps on trying to fulfill its manifest destiny. I don't mean that bellicose, bankrupt Manifest Destiny worked up by our politicians in the last century to justify territorial expansion, the betrayal of Indian treaties, and the assault on our common environment. I mean instead that hope of individual spiritual renewal that was implicit at the very moment Columbus's crews raised out of the wastes of night, ocean, and the blankness of their own charts the first faint outlines of the islands of the Antilles. Misguided though they were about the identity of the lands they had found, still these salt-studded men brought to the New World a special truth: the centuries of Old World longings for some new place—heavenly field, magic mountain, fortunate isle—in which to begin again, some place beyond human history where the presence of divinity would be daily evident in a landscape unmarked by human hands.

America, the actual place, was not that, of course. No earthly place could have been. However then unsuspected, it too had its history, its human inhabitants, and so it too had been marked here and there by restless human ingenuity. The first-coming whites found the island tribes, their boats, weirs, huts, and settlements, and then, inland, the astonishing cities of the Aztecs and Incas. Still, the great land was magnificent of aspect and pristine enough to permit the hungry intruders to continue in that hope of renewal, however much it became for them obscured by blood, rapacity, and the piecemeal carving of the environment.

In what became known as North America, that hope took on a strange quality with the coming of the Puritans to Massachusetts early in the seventeenth century. For while these God-haunted seekers hoped as had others before them to meet divinity here and so to be renewed, they regarded their

10

portion of the New World as a horrid place of exile, harkening back to Old Testament images of the Palestinian desert wherein an earlier chosen people had been tested and found wanting. It may be, thought John Winthrop, surveying the worn-out Old World he was leaving behind and that "desert" on which he had fastened his hopes for salvation, that "God will by this meanes bringe us to repent of our Intemperance here at home, and so cure us of that disease, which sendes many amongst us to hell. So he carried his people into the wildernesse, and made them forgett the fleshepottes of Egipt, which was some pinch to them indeed, but he disposed it to their good, in the ende." If renewal was to be had here, it would be *despite* the American landscape, not because of it. The unhallowed land was trial, not deliverance, and in the wake of the Puritans' example, the American land would look different, less like potential Eden, more like stubborn soil from which the enterprising might wrest some kind of victory. Henceforth American hope would have always to reckon with the Puritans' resistance to the land. Partly because of them, the old belief in America as the place of renewal moved westward ahead of actual settlement, toward the sun setting in the mountains — which could still harbor hope because they were mostly rumor.

Back in New England, that sliver of the continent they had made their own, the Puritans' nineteenth-century successors began to confront the new realities: stump fields, erosion, reduced flows in streams and rivers, the disappearance of the game and the extinction of species, and the primitive beginnings of an industrial system that, disturbingly, replicated that of the Old World. By the 1830s — scarcely two centuries after the Puritans came ashore at Plymouth and looted a cache of Indian corn, and less than three and a half centuries after Columbus in the Antilles had walked among the "loveliest trees" he had ever seen — it was possible for a solitary, musing white man out on the Great Plains, where the earth shook beneath the weight of the buffalo, to predict the end of the America that in its very wildness had so sponsored hope. George Catlin, moving alone through the tribes and vast herds with his notebook and paints, remarked with astonishing foresight on the need for a kind of park, recommending that some portion of what he now saw and painted be set aside from settlement and speculation. We have gotten territory enough, he thought, and predicted that future generations would come to appreciate some remnant of this wilderness saved out — like a sacred grove — from what he called the "march of civilization and death."

Catlin's voice was but one, and it was easily drowned out by those many more bellowing about the nation's Manifest Destiny. In such a cultural climate any talk of conservation sounded foolish. In the 1840s and fifties, as the eagle of nationalism began to flap and stretch its wings, only the American Transcendentalists took note of the fact that Americans' relationship to their lands had nothing of the original or renovative about it and that the conquest of the New World recapitulated in every significant detail that of the Old. Heirs of those European Romantics who had been forced to discover their voices in the somber shadows of smokestacks and slums, the Transcendentalists called upon Americans to take authentic possession of their lands by becoming possessed *by* them. But this "original" relationship with Nature, which Emerson claimed was the American national destiny, could hardly be achieved in a landscape as brutalized and built up as America seemed destined to become, a landscape from which divinity seemed to have been systematically purged, along with the tribes and the wild things, in the blind worship of the great god Progress. When Thoreau went to Walden Pond on Independence Day, 1845, it signified both a retreat from what America had become and also an attempt (the first of many such) imaginatively to rediscover America with new eyes and an open heart.

Few heeded Thoreau's example and only a few more Emerson and the other Transcendentalists. But when at length the relentless rush westward joined the Gold Rush to California, then the warnings of these American Romantics began to take on weight, for there was now left no geographical region in the states to which hope might safely be removed. Unwittingly, we had filled up our once imponderable spaces and in so doing had failed to discover their inmost promise for us.

Still there remained as a deep strain in the national character this impulse for hope, the abiding belief that, filled up or no, the American land had been meant for more than the simple making of money, that those first-comers had been right after all in imagining that America was a divinely vouchsafed second chance, however quickly they had botched it for themselves. How else are we to explain, for instance, those dozens of utopian communities and splinter sects that have taken root and briefly flowered in the American earth since the Puritans set up their city on a hill? Robert Owen's people in New Harmony, the Brook Farmers, the Mormons (moving steadily west toward hope), the Amana Society in Iowa, the Hutterites in South Dakota, Cyrus Teed's Koreshan community at Estero, Florida, and on into our own day with the followers of Bhagwan Shree Rajneesh at Antelope, Oregon: however much Main Street America might wish to disavow such movements and their adherents, their persistence down the centuries tells us that they are peculiarly in the mainstream of the American experience. So, too, are those dreamers, hermits, and cranks who have persisted in believing that America was meant to be the chosen place for the rebirth of the human spirit—Ann Lee, Thoreau, Emerson, John Brown, Walt Whitman, John Muir, Jane Addams, Woody Guthrie, Scott Nearing, Martin Luther King, Jr. . . .

A good case could be made, I think, that such individuals more accurately represent our most radical (as in root) Americanness than do those of Mount Rushmore's stone pantheon.

~

The conservation movement forms an important part of the history of hope here in America. That is its large context. Its more immediate one is that

Albert Bierstadt. Yosemite Valley. 1868. Oil on canvas. 36 x 54″. Oakland Museum, Gift of Marguerite Laird in memory of Mr. and Mrs. P. W. Laird. Photo: M. Lee Fatherree. The premier painter of the Far West, Bierstadt exhibited his heroic panoramas beginning in 1860 to a public hungry for information about America's recently surveyed natural wonders. "Why should our artists make their pilgrimages to the Alps for mountains, to Italy for skies, or to Chamouni valley, when we have the mountains and skies of California and the Valley of Yo-semite? This valley has some of the most remarkable scenery in the world," wrote a critic in 1865 about Bierstadt's series of paintings of the place.

"industrial democracy"—as the early nineteenth-century reformer Theodore Parker termed it—that exploded into being in the three decades following the Civil War, for it was out of this new cultural order that conservation's first leaders came.

In important respects, the war itself created the necessary conditions for the new order, not least because the fighting so sapped the nation's moral energy that, with the assassination of Lincoln, a great, penetrating hush fell over the land. That was to be expected in the flattened South, but in the North—the alleged victor—there were few leaders left who could now raise clear voices to inform and lead a weary people into a consideration of the great responsibilities victory imposed. The steam had been taken out of all the antebellum reform movements, and among the victors there was now an evident unease about what should be done with those dark others on whose ostensible behalf the bloody crusade had been waged. Many of the great antebellum voices had been stilled by death or age, weariness or public neglect: Parker, Whittier, Whitman, Melville, Thoreau, Emerson. "We had hoped," said Emerson, speaking for the antebellum reformers, that "after such a war, a great expansion would follow in the mind of the country; grand views in every direction. . . . But the energy of the nation seems to have expended itself in the war." Those who had hoped the war might act as a mighty purge, after which America would be free to fulfill its moral destiny, now lived to witness the failure of Reconstruction and the rise of men whose only real hope was the acquisition of great wealth. War, said Lewis Mumford in his survey of these postwar years he called the "Brown Decades," does not bring heroism, fortitude, or a concern for one's fellows into the subsequent peace. Instead, "it merely prepares a richer soil for the civilian's vices. One might as well expect a high sense of tragedy in an undertaker, as heroism in the generation that follows a war. . . ."

In this moral and spiritual interregnum, the lands of the public domain in the defeated South and those far vaster federal holdings in the West were opened to settlement and the private exploitation of their natural resources of soil, timber, and minerals. A transcontinental rail system was completed. Tall tariff walls were erected to shield fledgling industries, and the nation's doors were flung wide to the millions of immigrants who would work in these industries and live in the ever-expanding cities. For the first time in our history, huge inequities in wealth, political power, and social influence became conspicuous and tolerated features of the national life, and the millionaire, numbered in the few hundreds before the war, became a hero, his numbers now in the thousands. On all this—the making of the American world we know—state legislatures and the federal government smiled complacently, unwilling to interfere lest they "minimize" the citizen and "maximize" the government, as a Missouri court put it in 1898 in a grotesque wrenching of eighteenth-century political theory. And the clergy, before the war such a potent force for reform, now devoted a telling portion of its efforts to explaining to congregations how perfectly the laws of laissez-faire

capitalism accorded with those of the Almighty.

Of all these developments, it seems clear now that the one with the greatest lasting consequences has been the unchecked despoilment of the American environment. The great issues faced by the new industrial democracy—civil rights, the rights of women and of workers, public education and health—might be addressed (and remedied) by the ballot, by legislation, by protest, or by the creation of trade unions and kindred special interest organizations. But, as we have had to learn at great cost, to clean up or restore an environment is a far more resistant matter. For twenty years following Appomattox few voiced real concern about what was happening to the American earth and what the multiple consequences of its ravagement might be. Even fewer looked ahead and asked what America would be like when all its wild places had been brought under the dominion of machines and their makers.

By the time of the Centennial celebration this seemed the nation's fate, and so it was fitting that the celebration's centerpiece should be the 680-ton Corliss steam engine on view in Philadelphia. Regarding it with rueful admiration, William Dean Howells, intellectual descendant of the silenced Romantics, was forced to conclude that it perfectly expressed the national genius. Where Emerson had claimed that Americans were called to develop an original relationship with Nature, men like George Corliss of Providence had come forward to harness Nature's powers and force them to turn the wheels of enterprise. That, evidently, was to be the character of our original relationship with Nature. "Nature's nation," we had been accustomed to styling ourselves. Now we might well call ourselves "machinery's men," brought by our energy and ingenuity to a psychological threshold of such significance that to cross it might involve nothing less than a reinvention of America. For the land was being used up at such a fearsome rate that it was possible to foresee (as Catlin had in the 1830s) a not-distant time when most of our national resources would be plundered and the last fragments of wilderness entered upon and exploited. Then America would be nothing more than the counterpart of the Old World that Columbus had left behind and whose "Satanic mills" had formed so powerful an emotional antithesis since Jefferson's time. If, as had long been claimed, American nature was the new nation's special fund of virtue, its true lode, what then of an America, prematurely aged, where nature had been pillaged and paved and the West was but another name for "civilization"? How then to think of America and from what farther range to draw hope?

Fortunately for us who have inherited the American world made in these brown decades, men and women now began to appear on the national scene who had a care for the future, our present. Reformers along a variety of lines, those with the greatest claim to our continuing gratitude were the ones who concerned themselves with the environment: George Perkins Marsh, Henry George, Frederick Law Olmsted, George Bird Grinnell, Theodore Roosevelt, Charles Sprague Sargent, C. Hart Merriam, Gifford Pinchot, Robert Underwood Johnson, and John Muir, whose life and thought continue to form the bole of the American environmentalist tree.

༻

Singular though he seems, Muir was in many important respects classically American. His life would have made sense to Benjamin Franklin and to Henry Thoreau. It made perfect sense to Emerson, who met Muir in Yosemite in 1871. And later, Theodore Roosevelt paid tribute to Muir as the highest type of American citizen. In our time, Muir seems to many in the global environmental movement an example of the very best American culture can produce: an eccentric, self-made man who discovered how to translate his profound love of the American earth into practical actions to protect it.

To begin with, there was the immigrant experience, Muir and his family in 1849 joining the tide of seekers that had steadily built during that decade. Like many who then came here, Muir was short on formal education, but he was long on intellectual initiative, and the education he provided for himself in the long hours of self-designed study proved infinitely better than the best then available at American institutions. Without understanding much about the adopted culture he would have to enter, Muir in the isolation of the family's Wisconsin farm fitted himself, Franklin-like, to act many parts: farmer, mechanic, teacher, inventor, factory supervisor, polemicist, lobbyist, author. In the course of his life he was all of these, often brilliantly so. But the part he played best was that of the solitary tramp who derived inspiration and unquenchable hope from his intimate acquaintance with the land. Here, truly, was the highest promise of America realized.

He apprenticed for this part while still a schoolboy in Dunbar, Scotland, when with his unruly fellows he ran the roads through the Lammermuir Hills and wandered the rocky coast past Long Craigs toward Behaven Bay. Childhood's play here, surely, and yet in his sunset years Muir looked back on those childhood excursions and was certain they had announced the beginnings of his love affair with the natural world. The apprenticeship continued on the Wisconsin farm when he would devise occasional and precious escapes from his father's dictatorship to wander in hardwood groves or roam the night-blessed fields.

By the time of the Civil War, Muir was deeply and forever in love with the land. The sentiment was native, largely untutored, and he had surely earned it the hard way; any lover of the natural world who has had a farm upbringing will attest to that. But by now he had the Romantics, too, both European and home-grown varieties, and these writers heartened him on his way. At the state university at Madison he was introduced to Emerson's

Albert Bierstadt. Inyo County, California. n.d. Oil on panel. 17 x 21⅛″. Sierra Club Archives, on loan to the Oakland Museum. Photo: M. Lee Fatherree. Bierstadt based his spectacular paintings of the Sierra Nevada on sketches he made outdoors on trips West in 1859, 1863, and 1871. Drawn to wilderness, he camped in Yosemite for seven weeks and explored Hetch Hetchy Valley to the north as well as Kings Canyon. The works he later produced in his New York studio ranged from mural-sized canvases and easel paintings, such as this one, to designs for engravings and chromolithographs. Such prints satisfied clients with modest budgets, as did the similarly composed photographs of Yosemite by Carleton E. Watkins, Eadweard Muybridge, and Charles L. Weed, examples of which are reproduced here.

works and almost certainly also to Thoreau's; both would prove lasting and powerful influences. When in 1893 and already beginning to look like an American legend in his own right, Muir visited Walden Pond for the first time, he felt he had returned home. More precisely and indelibly than anyone before John Muir, Thoreau had expressed the essential American equation: in wildness is the preservation of the world, and wherever we encounter nature unimproved, *there* is America still.

Muir missed the war, believing like many another immigrant that it was not his affair and feeling no need to assist in that cause that had enlisted the passions of Emerson, Thoreau, and other antebellum reformers. Instead, he spent the years 1863–66 wandering in Canadian woods and bogs, returning briefly to civilization at Indianapolis before disappearing again from the life of his times to engage himself in a study of the land that was at once comprehensive and microscopic, mystical and analytic. When, in the mid-1870s, he came down from the Sierra, it was to do battle with what Emerson had called the "demagogues in the dusty arena below," lending his voice and his vision to the beginnings of the American environmental movement.

Muir was not by nature political, nor was he a joiner. He had always kept himself outside the mainstream of American affairs and had not even bothered to become a citizen of his adopted country (nor would he until 1903), pursuing a way as solitary as it was inspired, as if he traveled always in forest groves far removed from the petty strivings of the humans below. But as isolated as he had contrived to make himself, he was nevertheless a keen observer of American environmental developments, and as the 1890s came on he could not have missed the impressive sense that much more was ending now than just the nineteenth century. In some way that defied precise definition, an end seemed imminent for the New World as it had been known for centuries. In 1890 the brand-new state of Wyoming declared a ten-year closed season on buffalo, a prohibition that would have seemed foolishly unnecessary but ten years earlier. In South Dakota, itself a brand-new state, Sitting Bull, the last major figure of tribal resistance, was murdered at his home, sparking the massacre at Wounded Knee, which ended three centuries of Indian wars. The census of 1890 officially noted the disappearance of that frontier that had always been the most conspicuous feature of the American psychological landscape. And in Washington and Chicago planning continued for the mammoth celebration marking the four hundredth anniversary of Columbus's landfall in the Antilles. In view of these and kindred phenomena, it might be that Muir now began to think in terms of strategy and association in defense of the environment. That would explain why he was receptive when Robert Underwood Johnson had suggested in

1889 a campaign for a Yosemite National Park and why Muir was similarly receptive to Johnson's suggestion later in the same year that some kind of nature association be formed with Muir at its head.

The suggestion bore fruit in the spring of 1892 with the founding of the Sierra Club, but exactly what kind of club this was to be nobody then was quite certain. Some of its founders and charter members evidently thought of it as primarily an outing club. Some thought of it as a Yosemite watchdog organization, and Muir himself apparently thought it might be useful in this way. As for his long-range hopes for the new club, the most we can say with confidence is that Muir believed that if its members got out into the mountains and received the "good tidings," they might then be enlisted as Nature's protectors and spokesmen. But in that spring of '92, neither he nor any of

William Keith. Headwaters of the San Joaquin. 1878. Oil on canvas. 40 x 72". Oakland Museum, Gift of the Keith Art Association. Photo: M. Lee Fatherree. William Keith was a longtime resident of Berkeley and painted the Sierra from years of experience. He was a close friend of John Muir (they are portrayed together with naturalist John Burroughs on p. 78) and illustrated some of his articles.

the other founders could have imagined how swiftly the amorphous new club would have to become an aggressive and politically adroit activist organization.

Yet this was in truth the nature of the Sierra Club's first challenge, for no sooner had Yosemite become a national park, joining Yellowstone as part of that "geography of hope" (as Wallace Stegner put it), than it came under the threat of dismemberment. Under pressures from timber, mining, and livestock interests, a bill was introduced in Congress that would drastically shrink the park's dimensions. Eventually, the bill died in committee, and Muir judged the park was safe, "at least for this time." But in this relatively undramatic first battle lay implicit most of the important lessons the Sierra Club and the American environmental movement would relearn piecemeal over the next century.

First, no piece of American land, however sanctified by historical association, popular regard, or binding legislation is ever utterly safe from development. All of it—*all*—is potentially real estate, and as the land reformer Henry George pointed out in 1879, there is a progressive, ineluctable tendency for the value of undeveloped land to rise as population grows and settlement expands. Many of the most heated, protracted battles the Sierra Club has fought in its first hundred years — from Hetch Hetchy Valley north of Yosemite at the beginning of the century to today's fight to preserve the Everglades — have been on behalf of sites already supposedly reserved from development forever. But as the population of urban and suburban areas has continued to expand, so have the perceived needs of the people, until at last the unthinkable becomes thinkable and indeed feasible. By the time of the First World War, it was clear that no American lands would necessarily remain national forests or national parks or wilderness areas or monuments for which some new need had been discovered. This persistent condition of threat is one the Sierra Club has had to learn to live with, just as it has learned to live with the corollary accusation that it is an enemy of progress.

The Club learned a cognate lesson from the first Yosemite battle: no environmental war is ever finally won, though any battle, when lost, is lost forever. Muir evidently suspected this when he said Yosemite was safe for the time being. But if the Sierra Club thought the Yosemite war was finished in 1905, it learned shortly that what it had really been engaged in was an endless campaign of which its victories had been but parts. The Hetch Hetchy conflict of 1901–14 showed the Club the actual dimensions of the contest, and with the flooding of the valley that part of the war would seem forever lost. Similarly today, while the Everglades jetport proposal is dead, no one aware of the tremendous pressures on that park believes this defeat means the end of the war: the Everglades remains in the cross-hairs.

Third, the Yosemite battle and the subsequent, nationally publicized conflict over Hetch Hetchy proved the need for a precise understanding of the way the federal government actually operated, for an active presence in the nation's capital, and for the development of pressure tactics that could work on politicians' ambitions when appeals to their consciences failed.

The Sierra Club's defeat at Hetch Hetchy was really the defeat of amateurism in the environmental war. Then it was realized that no one person, nor even a cadre, could hope to understand how things now were done, how many were the tactics of those who had their eyes on a piece of undeveloped land, how patient they could be. Henceforth, it would be seen as the task of politically and legally savvy Club members, like later officers Bestor Robinson, Richard M. Leonard, David Brower, and Michael McCloskey, to keep abreast of an increasingly labyrinthine federal bureaucracy and to devise their own means (like the Sierra Club Foundation, The Sierra Club Legal Defense Fund, and the Club's Political Committee) for meeting the new challenges.

The fourth lesson of Yosemite was the great one, and it emerged only gradually. When the battle was over, the bill dead, and the park safe for the time being, it seemed as if a victory had been won for California nature lovers. In fact, as we have come to understand, a victory had been won for nature itself.

Nature, as Muir — and Thoreau before him — observed, cannot speak with the tongues of humankind. It might even be said that for most humans

Gilbert Munger. Yosemite Valley Scene. 1876. Oil on canvas. 20 x 28". Oakland Museum, City Acquisition Fund Purchase

nature cannot speak at all, except in the terrible syllables of outrage, as in natural disasters. But this does not mean that nature is dumb; only that we are dumb to it. When we come close enough to nature anywhere, Muir taught, we are enabled to hear its speech, which is really a song of existence. Long before anyone dared write of the "rights of nature," John Muir said that any natural object had the right to exist, simply because it had its own being, its own history, its own motives and purpose. What was saved in the first Sierra Club battle was a park for Californians to enjoy, for Americans to glory in. But more significantly, what was saved were the natural objects of that park, *saved to be themselves*. That in time has become a precious principle and one the Club has successfully given to the global environmental movement.

That this principle should be a gift from an American organization to the global environmental movement is deeply appropriate, for the Sierra Club and the other organizations that have followed it continue to draw upon that reservoir of hope that has been a part of our national character since the days of first discovery. Despite the many disappointments in the five centuries since Columbus, our multiple, repeated, individual, and collective failures to be equal to the terrific beauty of this place and to the Everest-high ideals set forth in our founding documents — despite, in short, what we have thus far made of the great second chance — Americans still hope. They hope for themselves that the chance for renewal may yet be realized. And they hope that America, the nation, may one day live its destiny of providing authentic liberty and classless justice. This, finally, is what distinguishes us from other nations, though it does not make us first among them, a concept as bankrupt as the old Manifest Destiny. The locus of that hope was in the beginning the American land. It still is.

— Frederick Turner

PREFACE
AND
ACKNOWLEDGMENTS

❧

Mountains have beckoned people since the beginning of time. Indian spirits live in them. So do the gods of the ancient Greeks. It should not be surprising, therefore, that it was love of mountains that first brought together the men and women who created an organization that would one day dedicate itself to the preservation of the entire earth.

The Sierra Club, born and raised in California, the brainchild of an Easterner and a transplanted Scot, celebrates its hundredth birthday in May of 1992; this book celebrates the Sierra Club.

Founded by twenty-seven Californians in a lawyer's office in San Francisco in 1892, the Club has grown to over six hundred and fifty thousand members, who reside in all states of the Union, all the provinces of the Canadian confederation, and most member-nations of the United Nations. Its first group or committee of members outside San Francisco (called a "chapter") was established in 1911 in Los Angeles; today it has fifty-seven chapters, which are subdivided into 370 groups. The Club's first field office—a one-man affair—was opened in 1961 in Eugene, Oregon, to further the Club's conservation work in the Pacific Northwest. Today there are field offices in fourteen cities and towns, in addition to a lobbying office in Washington, D.C., staffed by thirty people. The outings program, begun in Yosemite in 1901 for members to have fun, to educate them, and to recruit new ones, now sponsors three hundred trips each year, to twenty countries, trips enjoyed by some four thousand people. Chapters sponsor another estimated eight thousand outings each year. The staff has grown from one cabin custodian and information provider at the end of the nineteenth century to 250 employees in 1990.

The Club's areas of interest have grown likewise, from enjoyment and protection of the mountains of California and the Pacific Coast to a broad concern for the natural and human environment throughout the world. Today the Club, through its professional staff and its tens of thousands of volunteer members, tackles ecological problems ranging from clear-cutting in national forests to the contamination of groundwater with poisonous chemicals, from the restoration of degraded marshes to the rescue of endangered species. Though the board of directors makes a heroic attempt to keep the agenda organized and manageable, the Club's concerns are virtually infinite.

It is daunting, to put it mildly, to undertake a biography of so venerable, celebrated, and controversial an organization as the Sierra Club. Many books have been written and published that deal with the Club's history, either as the main focus or as part of another story. I have borrowed liberally from them all. For readers who would like to pursue the subject further, I direct them to the list of selected sources on page 282.

This is not a critical analysis of the Sierra Club then and now. It is, rather, a general history of the organization, told partly in words, partly in pictures. The Club's archive is rich in historic photographs, and its book division has published the work of many of America's major landscape photographers of the past several decades. This book presents samples of both recent and not-so-recent photography to give an impression of the century that has passed for the Club since it was born.

The text mentions some of the scrapes the Club got into and how it got out of most of them in time. It does not dwell on the squabbles that have flared within the organization now and again but recounts the successes with greater relish.

If one thing sets the Sierra Club apart from its kindred organizations, it is the way each member, each active member at least, feels that he or she is part owner of the institution. The Club is the most democratic such organization in existence, with literally thousands of committees that decide policy, strategy, and tactics on a vast range of topics large and small. It has been estimated that there are upwards of six thousand Club members who bear one official title or another.

This sort of democratic ownership of governing institutions is not without its drawbacks, of course. It can make decision-making slow, meetings long and ponderous. When the structure works well, however, it supports a strong, stable, unified organization that can accomplish great feats.

The Sierra Club can claim a good many such feats after its first hundred years of trying. May the next hundred be even better.

For assistance and guidance in preparation of this text I am grateful to Mike McCloskey, Joanne Hurley, Phoebe Adams, Helmi Nock, Carl Pope, Rich Hayes, John DeCock, Doug Scott, and Jon Beckmann of the Club staff; former Club presidents Edgar Wayburn, Richard M. Leonard, and Richard Cellarius; to Wheaton Smith of the Outing Committee; to Diana Landau, who helped select and edit the photographs and gave invaluable editorial guidance; to Anne Hoy of Harry N. Abrams, Inc., who edited the manuscript with patience and understanding and made the final selection of the photographs with Abrams' Ray Hooper, who provided the book's handsome design; and, most of all, to Dave Brower, the Club's first executive director, who brought me into the conservation movement as a passionate supporter in 1965 and as a full-time employee in 1968, opened his personal library and archive to me, and reviewed the manuscript and offered many useful suggestions.

— Tom Turner

MAKING THE MOUNTAINS GLAD

❧

JOHN MUIR,
THE BIRTH OF THE SIERRA
CLUB, AND THE FIGHT FOR
HETCH HETCHY VALLEY
AND YOSEMITE NATIONAL
PARK

1838 ❧ 1914

It has been argued, with considerable justice, that one of the two or three most valuable American contributions to world civilization is the national park idea. Setting aside large tracts of wilderness, to be preserved and protected for all citizens for all time, is an idea that sprang from the American earth in the mid-nineteenth century, one that has since been adopted by scores of other nations. If Henry David Thoreau was right, that "in wildness is the preservation of the world," then our national parks and other wilderness reserves may turn out to be our salvation, both physically and psychologically. For it is within those reserves that nature lives on, more or less untainted by the effluvia of modern society. And wilderness, as Nancy Newhall wrote with such insight in *This Is the American Earth,* "holds answers to more questions than we yet know how to ask." We obliterate it at our peril.

The parks and reserves created in the decades following the birth of the national park idea at Yosemite were carved from an America that was still largely wilderness. The creators of the parks, including John Muir, founder of the Sierra Club, had the vision to understand that wilderness would one day become a dwindling resource: one can only be grateful for the incisiveness of that vision.

❧

JOHN MUIR AND HIS MISSION

In 1868 John Muir alighted from a steamer in San Francisco, after a long, sometimes difficult journey from the Gulf of Mexico to Cuba to the Isthmus of Panama and on to California's booming gold-rush town. He was thirty years old.

Muir was born in Dunbar, Scotland, on April 21, 1838, and early in life developed a passionate love for wilderness. "When I was a boy in Scotland,"

Muir wrote later, "I was fond of everything that was wild, and all my life I've been growing fonder and fonder of wild places and wild creatures."[1]

There were seven children in the Muir family, three boys and four girls. The father was a bible-thumping shopkeeper but not a very successful businessman. When John was eleven, the Muirs packed up and sailed for America to begin a new life. They wound up in the woods of Wisconsin, ten or twelve miles from the town of Portage, and turned to a life of farming. John would do the backbreaking work of a farm laborer for eight years.

During this period, his adolescence, Muir read whatever he could find, mainly books borrowed from neighbors. Though his father distrusted any literature that was not the Bible or a learned analysis of it, he tolerated books on science, and young John read and absorbed a good deal of knowledge about mathematics, geology, and the life sciences. He also defied his father and spirited books of English Romantic poetry into the house, finding in himself, according to several biographers, a resonance with the writers' musings about nature and humanity's role in it.[2] This would prove to be a powerful influence on him throughout his life.

John Muir, by all accounts, was good at just about everything. Early on he exhibited a flair for invention. At the age of fifteen he built a sawmill powered by the stream that ran through the family homestead. He made a clock without ever having had the advantage of seeing the real item. He built a thermometer from bits of metal he found around the farm.

At the age of twenty-two and at the urging of a neighbor, Muir went off to the state fair at Madison with some of his inventions. They were a sensation. He won a prize of fifteen dollars and decided to leave home for intellectual pursuits. He enrolled in the University of Wisconsin. It was 1861.

Records from this period are scarce, but biographers think Muir studied botany, geology, Latin, and literature at the university for about two and a half years. This was during the Civil War, and in the spring of 1863 Congress approved a draft for all men between the ages of twenty and forty-five.

Riots swept the country. Some objected to war as a matter of principle. Others disagreed with the Union's position. Others, exhibiting a more racist sentiment, did not want to go to war on behalf of slaves. Many recent immigrants—including a good number in Wisconsin—simply felt that this was not their war, that they had not uprooted themselves from their ancestral lands in order to fight someone else's battles thousands of miles from home. Draft dodging was extremely common.

In 1864 Muir went to Canada to avoid being drafted. His reasons are not altogether clear, but in any event he joined thousands of his contemporaries who refused to fight. He remained until the war was over, evidently spending much time studying the natural landscape. He then returned to the United States and found factory work in Indianapolis. It looked as if he might make a successful career as an inventor and manufacturer, but one day, as he was working on a machine, he accidentally stabbed himself in the right eye. Then his left eye ceased to see, in evident sympathy with its counterpart, and he was blind for a time.

Muir was terrified. After his sight slowly returned over several weeks, he decided he would devote the balance of his life to the study and enjoyment of what mattered most to him: wild nature. He would see as much of the world as he could, and learn as much as possible about it. He took off by rail for Louisville, Kentucky, and then, on foot, to the Gulf of Mexico. He planned to continue from there to South America, studying plants and animals as he went. To the everlasting benefit of American wilderness, his plan went awry. He sailed to Cuba, but he could not find passage to South America. He sailed to New York, then found a ship bound for Panama. He traveled by train across the Isthmus and caught a boat headed for San Francisco.

Muir disembarked in San Francisco in 1868, and, according to his own account, asked the first person he saw the quickest way out of town. "Where do you want to go?" asked the man. "To any place that is wild," Muir replied. He was directed to the wharf and the ferry to Oakland, across the bay to the east.

He didn't want to go to just any place, in fact. In the late 1850s Muir had read the first magazine stories about the fabulous Yosemite Valley and the nearby giant sequoias, and it was toward them he set out. From Oakland, he walked south along the bay, up the Santa Clara Valley, then turned east across the coast range at Pacheco Pass. From the crest of the ridge he beheld the great central valley and the distant mountains for the first time. He was deeply impressed.

> Looking eastward from the summit of the Pacheco Pass one shining morning, a landscape was displayed that after all my wanderings still appears as the most beautiful I have ever beheld. At my feet lay the

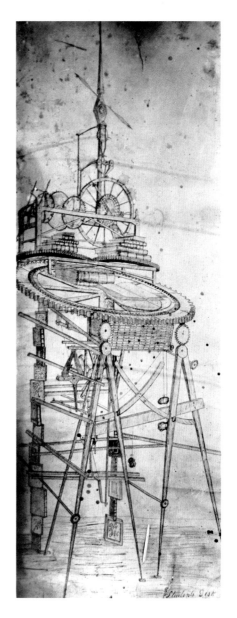

John Muir. Design for a study desk, drawn while he was at the University of Wisconsin. c. 1862. Sierra Club Archives

ABOVE

Carleton E. Watkins. Galen Clark and the Grizzly Giant. n.d. Gelatin silver print. 20 x 15″. Oakland Museum, Gift of the Women's Board of the Oakland Museum Association. Galen Clark first visited Yosemite in 1855, filed a claim for 160 acres on the Merced River in 1856, and discovered and named the Mariposa Grove of Big Trees in 1857. He was Guardian of the Yosemite Valley and the Grove in 1866–80 and 1889–96; his Wawona Station welcomed travelers entering the Valley from the south. A charter member of the Sierra Club, he is buried in Yosemite's Pioneer Cemetery.

RIGHT

Attributed to Charles Leander Weed. Yo-Semite Valley, from the Mariposa Trail. c. 1863. Albumen print. 15¾ x 20¼″. Oakland Museum, Gift of Rod and Lynn Holt. Late nineteenth-century photographers were not above altering nature to improve their compositions: this pine, for example, has lost some of its branches. Carrying his forty-pound view camera and heavy glass-plate negatives, Weed was the first to photograph Yosemite, in 1859.

Great Central Valley of California, level and flowery, like a lake of pure sunshine, forty or fifty miles wide, five hundred miles long, one rich furred garden of yellow compositae. And from the eastern boundary of this vast golden flower-bed rose the mighty Sierra, miles in height, and so gloriously colored and so radiant, it seemed not clothed with light but wholly composed of it, like the wall of some celestial city. Along the top and extending a good way down, was a rich pearl-gray belt of snow; below it a belt of blue and dark purple, marking the extension of the forests; and stretching along the base of the range a broad belt of rose-purple; all these colors, from the blue sky to the yellow valley smoothly blending as they do in a rainbow, making a wall of light ineffably fine. Then it seemed to me that the Sierra should be called, not the Nevada or Snowy Range, but the Range of Light.[3]

He made his way to the mountains and to Yosemite, and he was not disappointed. "Yosemite is the grandest, most divine of all earthly dwelling places," he wrote later, "the Lord's mountain house." It was as if he was meant to find the place.

❧

"THE LORD'S MOUNTAIN HOUSE"

Yosemite Valley had been entered by whites for the first time in 1851, though there is strong evidence that explorers had gazed down into the valley as much as twenty years earlier. By the early 1850s, Indians of several tribes in the Mother Lode, the western foothills of the Sierra Nevada, and gold miners were coming into frequent conflict. The state ordered the Indians to surrender and move onto reservations. Several groups refused and took refuge in remote spots, including a band of Ahwahneechee in Yosemite Valley. Several of them were subsequently captured near the town of Mariposa and they led soldiers into the valley to apprehend their mates, all of whom had fled. It was on that occasion, so far as is known, that non-Indians first entered the valley.

Word of the place spread quickly and widely, of the stupendous waterfalls and towering cliffs of polished granite, the lush meadows and crystalline streams. A little more than a decade after its "discovery," at the urging of Frederick Law Olmsted, designer of Central Park in New York City, Congress and President Lincoln moved to preserve it in 1864, creating the "Yosemite Grant"—two parcels of land encompassing Yosemite Valley and the Mariposa Grove of giant sequoias to the south.

Many books, many historians, and many ordinary people will tell you that the first national park in the world was not Yosemite but Yellowstone. They are mistaken. The first was Yosemite, created by Congress and President Lincoln on June 29, 1864, eight years before Yellowstone was similarly set

Galen Rowell. Ponderosa Pine Grove,
Yosemite Valley, California. 1986

Carr Clifton. Coreopsis Dominates a Field in Avenales Wildlife Preserve, California. 1988. The vast expanses of wildflowers—"like a lake of pure sunshine"—that impressed Muir in 1868 in the Central Valley are suggested by this photograph in a wildlife preserve. Today the valley itself is a fabric of tilled fields, as seen in the photograph at left.

Galen Rowell. The High Sierra from the Central Valley on a Clear Winter Day, California. 1988 aside, its geothermal wonders forever protected from private development and exploitation.

Yosemite, it is true, was then called a reservation, not a national park, and Congress gave it over to the administration and protection of the State of California. The purposes for its preservation, however, were quite clearly national: the grant was given "upon the express conditions that the premises shall be held for public use, resort and recreation, [and] shall be held inalienable for all time." Yosemite was thus the first park set aside for the pleasure and benefit of all citizens of the nation. As Hans Huth has pointed out, "These terms implied that no profit was to be expected from the new institution. . . . What was really new about the grant was the fact that it served a strictly nonutilitarian purpose." Citing various letters and documents of the period, Huth concluded, "The way Yosemite had been handled made it quite evident that in spite of the fact that the grant was made to the state, the object of the grant was considered to be of nation-wide, if not of world-wide importance."[4]

There are a goodly number of people who care about which park came first, not least because of the reasons for their creation. Yosemite was set aside to preserve its beauty and its wildness; Yellowstone was originally set aside mainly to preserve its curiosities. If Yosemite is the ideal, the paragon, then other areas with outstanding scenic features and unique ecological communities — not just places with boiling mudpots and reliable geysers — have a chance of being preserved as national parks and wilderness areas.[5]

❧

MUIR IN YOSEMITE

Muir fell instantly in love with Yosemite and took the few jobs available to support his living there. He herded sheep in the high country (though he detested them and came to call them "hooved locusts" for the damage they did to alpine meadows), and he ran a small sawmill in the valley (milling only trees that had fallen of their own accord), as he occupied a small cabin at the foot of Yosemite Falls.

Muir spent most of the next seven years — from 1869 until 1875 — in Yosemite and in the high country above it. He explored with the rigor of a scientist, collecting plants, writing descriptions, and making dozens of sketches of flowers, rocks, streams, and trees. He also explored with the senses of an artist and poet and the sensibility of a mystic, musing in his journals on the overpowering, divine beauty all around him. He saw life everywhere, even in the rocks. He studied his surroundings, partly as isolated features and partly to learn how the elements interacted with each other.

He considered the role of people in the natural world and he wondered in 1875, "What is the human's part of the mountain's destiny?" This sense of humility, that human beings are only one small part of nature's design, would inform his work and that of the Sierra Club and the American environmental movement from then on.

Some thought him a bit mad. He was famous for traveling without blankets (too heavy), without even much food. He was content to sleep in a pile of pine boughs and subsist on tea and oatmeal for days at a time. Storms brought him into the wild country rather than driving him to shelter. He particularly enjoyed climbing high in a tree during the fiercest of storms, to wave back and forth and gaze enraptured at the tumult.

Muir the scientist was particularly interested in how Yosemite and other Sierra valleys had come to be sculptured in the way they are. The leading theory of the day, propounded by Josiah D. Whitney of the California Geological Survey,[6] who had led an exploration of the Sierra in the 1860s, was that a great cataclysm had occurred in prehistoric times and had literally dropped the bottom out of the spot where Yosemite now stood.

Something in that thesis bothered John Muir. He suspected that great glaciers, grinding slowly down the flanks of the range, were a more likely cause. On his long, solitary rambles through the mountains, he kept searching for a remnant glacier to back up his belief in the glacier-carved theory of the Sierra. One day in 1871, he happened upon the Lyell Glacier, at the headwaters of the Tuolumne River, the next major watershed to the north of Yosemite's Merced River. Muir carefully placed markers on the glacier and on immovable stones beside it. Months later he returned to unmistakable evidence that the glacier was slowly moving. He had his proof.

Muir was a religious taker of notes, a diary keeper, a sketcher of trees and flowers and rock formations and streams. Friends had often urged him to submit articles to magazines for publication, but he resisted, saying, "what I have nobody wants." The discovery of glaciation changed that. Muir decided to write up his thesis and submit it to the most influential newspaper of the day, Horace Greeley's *New York Tribune*. His essay was accepted and published as "Yosemite Glaciers," a most promising start for a budding author.

Muir continued writing for publication, publishing more semiscientific articles in popular magazines, the *Overland Monthly* in particular, and more technical pieces in the *American Journal of Science* and the *Proceedings* of the American Association for the Advancement of Science. Once the glaciation argument was settled in Muir's favor, he turned to articles about the trees and other flora and fauna of the Sierra, which were published by major literary magazines like *Harper's Weekly* and *Scribner's Monthly*.

It was the beginning of a long and distinguished literary career. Muir wrote enthusiastically about his mountains and scathingly about threats to them from loggers, miners, and especially sheepmen. His style was flowery and frequently given to personification of natural objects; with the Emersonian pantheism of the era, he considered everything alive: animal, vegetable, and mineral.

As Freeman Tilden wrote, in his breezy history of the national parks:

> Muir was the understanding, untiring, articulate press-agent of the Sierra. . . . It was when Muir was writing for the joy of setting himself down in homely particular that he could write delightfully. . . . When Muir was writing . . . to arouse in the minds of a nation of readers an

enthusiasm and solicitude for these Sierra treasures, he was not so artless. He frequently opened the word-faucet and let the flood loose — two adjectives for every noun, a verbal phalanx in which every clause was trained to march straight ahead, fire a tremendous salvo at the end, and disperse the enemy, galvanize the unappreciative, spread the good news of conservation to the world. It came out of the goodness of his great heart and from his passion to have these precious places understood and protected.[7]

Eadweard Muybridge. Pi-Wi-Ack, Valley of the Yosemite. 1872. Albumen print. Mammoth plate, 16¾ x 21½". Oakland Museum, Gift of Robert B. Honeyman, Jr. Photo: M. Lee Fatherree. Muybridge, today better known for his photographic studies of motion, won early fame for his photographs of Yosemite and from 1867 competed with Carleton E. Watkins in making prizewinning prints of the subject.

Muir's public style of writing might be considered overblown today, but it was just right then. He won a wide following throughout the literary spectrum; and, once he took up residence in San Francisco in the mid-1870s, he became friendly with some of the city's most prominent and influential citizens, including professors and newspapermen. He was considered a bit eccentric, but he was admired all the same for his intelligence, enthusiasm, and talent as a naturalist and writer. A particular friend was the artist William Keith, who would contribute many drawings to Muir's articles and would soon join Muir and the lawyer Warren Olney in extended conversations about the plight of their beloved mountains and what they could do about it.

In 1880, after a long courtship, Muir married Louie Strentzel, the daughter of a successful, German-born, Polish-educated doctor turned orchardist who lived in Martinez in the fertile delta of the Sacramento River, a town some twenty-five miles northeast of San Francisco. Muir moved to Martinez, be-

George R. King. Yosemite Valley from the Wawona Road. 1909. Sierra Club Archives

BELOW LEFT
Joseph N. LeConte. Nevada Falls from the side, Yosemite Valley. 1897. Sierra Club Archives

BELOW RIGHT
George R. King. Vernal Falls on the Merced River, Yosemite Valley. 1909. Sierra Club Archives

came expert and prosperous at growing fruit, and withdrew from the literary scene. For nearly a decade he applied himself to raising his fruit trees, rearing two daughters, and earning a living.

He still made frequent visits to the mountains, growing more and more disturbed at the destruction he saw being visited on forests, streams, and meadows by sheepmen and loggers. Still he walked mainly alone: it took Louie one visit to determine that such trips were not for her, particularly given the spartan style in which her husband preferred to travel.

Anon. The John Muir home in Martinez, Contra Costa County, California, is now a National Historic Site. n.d. Sierra Club Archives

~

THE BIRTH OF AN IDEA

In 1889, the Easterner Robert Underwood Johnson, an editor at *Century Magazine*—the successor to *Scribner's*—which had published many of Muir's articles, toured the West in search of authors and articles to publish, and he paid a call on Muir. Readers in the East were still hungry for information and inspiration about the West and its wilderness. It was the abstract as much as the concrete that caught the public's fancy about the West, the notion of the wild, free, open spaces that could make a city dweller forget the crowds and clangor of daily life. Johnson's object was to persuade Muir to resume writing for the magazine, and his timing was perfect. Muir had his business in order and had decided to devote the balance of his life to preaching the virtues of the Sierra in particular and wilderness in general to the public, in order to save them from the mercenary interests that were fast ruining both. In response to Johnson's entreaty, Muir suggested that they spend a night or two in Tuolumne Meadows, in the high country above Yosemite Valley.

Muir and Johnson inspected the meadows and woods and concluded that something drastic had to be done immediately to stop the ravaging of the area by sheep and cattle and loggers and miners. They made a pact, a rather audacious one it would seem in this day and age. If Muir would write two articles for the *Century* on the plight of the Yosemite backcountry, and issue a clarion call for help, Johnson would use his own influence to persuade Congress and the president to create a Yosemite National Park to surround and protect Yosemite Valley.

Twenty-five years before, it will be recalled, the Yosemite Grant—the valley and the Mariposa Grove of big trees—had been made the responsibility of the State of California, but the state's management since 1864 had resulted in considerable damage to the resources of the reserve. (By the 1880s there was a large, odoriferous hog pen in the valley, for example, and a commercial hay-raising operation.) Muir once observed to Johnson, "The love of Nature among Californians is desperately moderate, consuming enthusiasm [is] almost wholly unknown." There was no way that Muir and Johnson could recommend that the state manage the new park. Indeed, Muir was coming around to the view that the federal government ought to reclaim the Reservation from the State of California, an idea that would be fought over for a

decade and a half before it prevailed. Muir and Johnson determined to take their campaign for a national park to Washington, D.C., and, with Johnson's help, to enlist the support of influential people in the East to persuade Congress to act.

How much simpler things were in those days! Muir and Johnson hatched the Yosemite National Park idea in the summer of 1889. The park should be very large, they thought, encompassing all the basins of all the streams that pour into the valley and the watershed of the Tuolumne River as well, from its source downstream well beyond Hetch Hetchy Valley, a smaller, near carbon copy of Yosemite itself. California Congressman General William Vandever submitted the legislation creating Yosemite National Park. The State of California tried to have the bill amended to give administration of the expanded grant to itself, but in vain. California evidently did not find much sympathy among the legislators.

On October 1, 1890, a little more than a year after the idea was born at a Tuolumne Meadows campsite, President Benjamin Harrison signed the bill that created the park. It comprised 1,512 square miles, nearly a million acres in a giant doughnut surrounding the Valley, which was left in the hands of the State of California. All grazing and tree-cutting were forbidden in the national park, and the Army was set to patrolling it to prevent abuses. Some important land was excluded to the north of the park, as was the Mariposa Grove, which remained the responsibility of the State of California but was separated from the new national park by a thin slice of land.

Although logging was outlawed in Yosemite in 1890 when it was named a park, the cutting continued in nearby areas, as seen in these panoramas by Edward T. Parsons, taken on the 1904 High Trip, or annual Club outing, to Yosemite, Tuolumne Meadows, and Hetch Hetchy Valley. Above top, Camp 15, a logging camp. Below, members of the High Trip ride a logging train for part of the return trip from Hetch Hetchy to Yosemite Valley. Sierra Club Archives

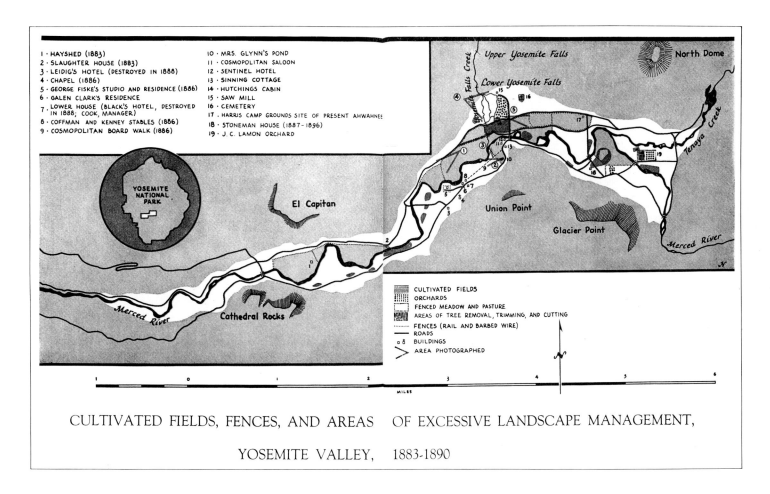

CULTIVATED FIELDS
ORCHARDS
FENCED MEADOW AND PASTURE
AREAS OF TREE REMOVAL, TRIMMING, AND CUTTING
FENCES (RAIL AND BARBED WIRE)
ROADS
BUILDINGS
AREA PHOTOGRAPHED

CULTIVATED FIELDS, FENCES, AND AREAS OF EXCESSIVE LANDSCAPE MANAGEMENT,

YOSEMITE VALLEY, 1883-1890

THE BIRTH OF AN ORGANIZATION

It was clear to all concerned, however, that simply naming some acres a national park and drawing a line on a map would not end the problems. Johnson had suggested, even before the national park bill became law, the idea of forming an association to defend Yosemite National Park. A contingent at the University of California had meanwhile come up with the idea of a club to sponsor educational and recreational outings into the Sierra. The history of this period is not altogether clear (the Sierra Club's records were destroyed in the fire that followed the earthquake of 1906), but these two groups got together, beginning in 1889. They spoke of creating an organization of citizens to keep pressure on the government to protect the park and to discourage attempts to have its boundaries shrunk at the behest of loggers, stockmen, and would-be dam builders, a counterattack that was to come all too soon.

At the same time, Muir, along with the university contingent in Berkeley, was strongly convinced that only people familiar with an area would be passionate defenders of it, and so he urged people to visit the high country, "to climb the mountains and get their good tidings," as he said.

There was some precedent for what soon emerged. Several groups had sprung up in the East with the principal mission of protecting specific areas

Map of Yosemite in 1883–90 showing fields, fences, and other evidence of cultivation. From Holway R. Jones, *John Muir and the Sierra Club: The Battle for Yosemite* (San Francisco: Sierra Club, 1965), 186–87.

OPPOSITE
Carleton E. Watkins. The Lower Yosemite Fall 418 Feet. c. 1861. Albumen print. Mammoth plate, 20⅜ x 15⅝". Oakland Museum, Gift of the Women's Board of the Oakland Museum Association. Photo: M. Lee Fatherree. Today as in their own time, Carleton E. Watkins is identified with Yosemite, as William Henry Jackson is with Yellowstone. Their photographs of these areas helped convince Congress to establish them as parks—an early instance of the political utility of photography. In their sublime conception and accomplished technique, the landscapes of Watkins and Jackson are intended to rival Hudson River School paintings: together, these works fostered the conception of the Far West as a promised land.

Anon. Portrait of Joseph LeConte. n.d.
Bancroft Library, University of California,
Berkeley. A geologist and protégé of the
great Louis Agassiz at Harvard, Joseph
LeConte was one of the first two scholars
hired by the University of California
following its founding in 1868. (His
brother John was the other.) Joseph was
a fervent mountaineer, and he led an
excursion of university personnel into the
Sierra Nevada in 1870, the account of
which became the Sierra Club's first
published book. He met John Muir that
same summer and was the first geologist
of international reputation to support
Muir's theory that Yosemite had been
carved by glaciers. LeConte was a
cofounder of the Sierra Club with Muir
and two dozen others, and he served on
its board until his death in 1898. He
camped every year in Yosemite, where
he died at age seventy-six, on the eve of
the first High Trip.

for their aesthetic and recreational qualities. One of the first was the Williamstown Alpine Club, founded in 1863 in Massachusetts. In the next decade three more regional organizations were founded—the White Mountain Club in Portland, Maine (1873), the Rocky Mountain Club in Colorado Springs (1875), and the Appalachian Mountain Club of Boston (1876). In the 1880s the first two wildlife preservation organizations were founded, the American Ornithological Union in 1883 and the first of many Audubon Societies in 1886. In 1887, Theodore Roosevelt and others founded the Boone and Crockett Club, an organization that promoted "manly sport with the rifle," to which end it would work "for the preservation of the large game of this country."

Boone and Crockett took as a principal duty the protection of Yellowstone National Park against various attempts to carve away parts of it and turn them over to private ownership and commercial enterprise. But representatives of Boone and Crockett, when asked if they would also take Yosemite under their wing, declined and suggested the formation of a new organization.

J. H. Senger and William Dallam Armes of the University of California at Berkeley sent formal invitations to attend a founding meeting for the new association. Muir responded enthusiastically, "Hoping that we will be able to do something for wildness and make the mountains glad."

Twenty-seven solid citizens met in the law office of Warren Olney on June 4, 1892, to sign legal incorporation papers.[8]

Muir was the unanimous choice for president. The purposes of the new organization, as stated in the Articles of Incorporation, would be: "To explore, enjoy, and render accessible the mountain regions of the Pacific Coast; to publish authentic information concerning them; and to enlist the support and cooperation of the people and government in preserving the forests and other natural features of the Sierra Nevada Mountains."

Founders included Muir and Warren Olney, J. H. Senger, and several other professors from Berkeley, including notably the geologist Joseph LeConte, who would serve the Club with distinction for many years. Another was the president of Stanford, David Starr Jordan. There were a couple of legislators and scientists from the U.S. Geological Survey. Most were scientists, scholars, or both. They were well-to-do but not wealthy, not of the class of the Hearsts or Chandlers, but from the part of the political spectrum that would come to be called "progressive." All had a fierce devotion to the Sierra and a determination to protect and defend it. The combination of scientific insight and an esthetic devotion to beauty and wilderness would characterize the new organization throughout its existence.

The new directors threw open the membership rolls of the organization and by September had enlisted 182 charter members, of whom several were women, including one of Muir's daughters, Wanda. There were many scholars from Berkeley and Stanford and scientists from government survey organizations. There were also doctors, lawyers, bankers, and others whose professions are now unknown.

A general meeting of members was called for September 16 in San

Francisco and 250 people turned out. Club Secretary William D. Armes described the creation of the Club and its objectives. R. M. Price told of a trip he had recently made down the Grand Canyon of the Tuolumne, the third person known to have done so. (The first two were Muir and Johnson.) Such recounting of mountain adventures was typical of early Club meetings and publications; members had a seemingly insatiable appetite for each other's experiences.

As a measure of the novelty and popularity of the new club, and of the public's interest in science and exploration, the second general meeting, a scant four weeks later, drew more than five hundred guests to hear Muir and Major John Wesley Powell. Powell had led the first party ever to float the Colorado River from Green River, Wyoming, to Grand Wash Cliffs at the bottom of the Grand Canyon, and he had later served as head of the U.S. Geological Survey. Powell was and remains a hero to conservationists for his science, his geographic discoveries, and his sound advice on the preservation of natural resources and scenery. His attitude toward rivers and water in the arid West was less popular. "All the waters of all the arid lands will eventually be taken from their natural channels" for irrigation, he had written in 1878.[9] This sentiment would serve as an unofficial motto for the federal Bureau of Reclamation, created in 1902, an agency that the Sierra Club would battle ferociously several decades later.

Three weeks later a third general meeting was held, and there the real work of the Sierra Club began.

Anon. Warren Olney, one of the Sierra Club's founding directors and the San Francisco attorney in whose offices the new Club signed its articles of incorporation. 1890s. California Historical Society, San Francisco

FIRST STEPS

Before September 1892 California Congressman Anthony Caminetti had already introduced a bill that would have drastically reduced the size of Yosemite National Park. It was done at the behest of lumber and mining interests. Professor Senger described the bill to Club members at their third meeting, and two speakers denounced it. The membership voted overwhelmingly to instruct the board of directors to prepare a petition to Congress—what was then known as a "memorial"—opposing the bill and to use every effort to defeat it.

After a slow start, the effort to redraw the boundaries of the park gathered some momentum, until Club Secretary and state legislator Elliott McAllister rallied his colleagues in Sacramento to oppose the Caminetti bill, which was twice voted down. (Caminetti's constituents solved the immediate problem by voting him out of office in 1896, but attempts to shrink the park would continue.)

Early in 1893 the first issue of the *Sierra Club Bulletin* (now known as *Sierra*) was published. Its early numbers are crammed with scientific reports and accounts of trips in the Sierra and other remote venues, in aid of the

Club's purposes of introducing people to the mountains and "publishing authentic information about them." They overflow with enthusiasm and the joy of discovery and adventure, of exploring places seldom (or never) visited by humans before. They are illustrated with black-and-white photographs and drawings and carry advertisements for climbing and camping equipment and railroads and stagecoach lines to desirable destinations.

Early *Bulletins* also present stories that describe some of the more onerous natural resource laws then on the books and exhort readers to implore Congress to repeal them. Much of this political work was left to Professor Charles Dudley of Stanford, who contributed a column called "Forestry Notes," which may have been the first attempt at the "grassroots lobbying" soon carried on by scores of organizations across the land. This enlisting of members in legislative campaigns would quickly become a hallmark of the Club, arguably its principal activity for the rest of its existence.

OPPOSITE
Christine Alicino. Still life of late nineteenth-century books about the Sierra by John Muir and others, from the Sierra Club Archives. 1991. It is reported that Muir never had a manuscript rejected by a publisher until he tried to sell his first book, *The Mountains of California*. The delay was minor, and the Century Company published it in 1894. The first printing sold out in a few months. Afterward came Muir's *Our National Parks*, 1901, a collection of articles he had written for the *Atlantic*, and then books based on his early journals, including *The Story of My Boyhood and Youth*, 1913; *The Yosemite*, 1914; *Travels in Alaska*, 1915; and *A Thousand Mile Walk to the Gulf*, 1916—the last two books published posthumously.

Dudley campaigned diligently for the repeal of what he called the "Three Dangerous Laws": the Desert Lands Act, the commutation clause of the Homestead Act, and the Timber and Stone Act, all of which were hastening the turning over of publicly owned lands to private interests, especially forest lands and lands suitable for grazing. He argued in favor of delegating management of the federal forest reserves (later to be called national forests) to the Department of Agriculture. He discussed and analyzed proposals for new parks and reserves.

In the early 1890s there were fewer than five hundred Sierra Club members, mainly in the Bay Area. All work was done by volunteers. The heaviest expenses were for rent ($135 a year for a small office in downtown San Francisco) and for printing the semi-annual *Bulletin* and maps and occasional reports.

In 1894 the Century Company published John Muir's first book, *The Mountains of California*, to enthusiastic notices. Muir's idea was to recruit new supporters to the cause of Sierra conservation and the defense of Yosemite. The Sierra Club was not yet in the book publishing business, though that would come soon enough and turn into one of the organization's most important activities.

In 1895 the Club held its first official annual meeting. Muir gave one of the warm, humorous talks that had brought him so many admirers. He must have exuded the aura of wilderness, with his trim, erect carriage, his ragged beard and faraway gaze. He began by disclaiming his qualifications as a speaker, suggesting that the serious business of conservation was "lawyer's work" and ought better be left to the vice president, Warren Olney.

There was plenty of such work at hand. Congressman Caminetti's efforts to reduce the size of Yosemite National Park have been mentioned. A giant Sierra Forest Reserve created by President Harrison in 1893 was being logged and grazed without restriction. Muir touched on those serious matters and claimed facetiously that his skills were unequal to them.

> You know that I have not lagged behind in the work of exploring our
> grand wildernesses, and in calling everybody to come and enjoy the

Carr Clifton. Tuolumne Meadows at Sunset, Yosemite National Park, California. 1985

thousand blessings they have to offer. I have faithfully inspected gorges, glaciers, and forests, climbed mountains and trees, and lived with the wild animals, and, as best I could, I have talked and written about them, never sparing myself. But this was not considered enough by the directors. More still was required of me. I must make speeches and lead in society affairs. This, as it appears to me, is not reasonable. This formal, legal, unwild work is out of my line.

He then reported a recent visit to the national park, where he investigated the condition of the backcountry and found it much improved over previous visits, before the park was created.

This last summer . . . I rambled off for an easy six weeks' saunter in the Sierra above Yosemite, and about the headwaters of the Tuolumne, and down the Grand Canon of the Tuolumne to Hetch Hetchy and the sugar-pine woods of the main forest belt. On this ramble I was careful to note the results of the four years of protection the region had enjoyed as a park under the care of the Federal Government, and I found them altogether delightful and encouraging. When I had last seen the Yosemite National Park region, the face of the landscape in general was broken and wasted, like a beautiful human countenance destroyed by some dreadful disease. Now it is blooming again as one general garden, in which beauty for ashes has been granted in fine wild measure. The flowers and grasses are back again in their places as if they had never been away, and every tree in the park is waving its arms for joy. . . .

Blessing on Uncle Sam's blue-coats! In what we may call homeopathic doses, the quiet, orderly soldiers have done this fine job, without any apparent friction or weak noise, in the still, calm way that the United States troops do their duty. . . .

He reminded his audience of the creation of Yosemite National Park in 1890 and of the struggle that had been necessary to preserve its boundaries intact.

The battle we have fought, and are still fighting, for the forests is a part of the eternal conflict between right and wrong, and we cannot expect to see the end of it. I trust, however, that our Club will not weary in this forest well-doing. The fight for the Yosemite Park and other forest parks and reserves is by no means over; nor would the fighting cease, however much the boundaries were contracted. Every good thing, great and small, needs defense.[10]

Muir's words were typically eloquent and prophetic: the Club would continue to dedicate itself to the preservation and enjoyment of the country's great and small places.

WILL COLBY
AND THE FIRST OUTINGS

In 1898 the Club's directors decided it would be wise to have a permanent Club presence in Yosemite, to assist visitors and to help the authorities keep damage checked. William E. Colby, a young mining lawyer from the Bay Area, took the job and moved to Yosemite Valley in 1898, taking up residence in a cabin owned by the Club on the valley floor.

Inspired by Muir's writings, Colby had visited the Sierra for the first time in 1894 at the age of nineteen. He encountered members of the Sierra Club and soon became a member. He had graduated from Hastings College of the Law in 1898 and spent the following summer as the Sierra Club's voice in Yosemite. It was the beginning of a long and very close relationship: Colby was appointed Club secretary in 1900, and he served on the Club's board for forty-nine years, two as president, the rest as secretary. For the sixteen years following his first association with the organization, Colby was one of Muir's closest confidants, playing the practical lawyer to Muir's visionary leader.

Colby's first major contribution to the Sierra Club was his invention of the High Trip. Following the successful fending-off of attempts to reduce the size of the park in the mid-nineties, club membership had slipped back to under four hundred in 1900 (from a previous high of about twice that number), possibly because the Club was no longer involved in a public battle on a regular basis and therefore not appearing in newspapers with so much regularity. As a way to build the organization, Colby suggested that it sponsor an annual trip into the High Sierra to knit club members closer together, introduce them to the mountains first hand, and recruit and retain more defenders of forest and stream. Muir endorsed the plan wholeheartedly.

Club policy had always been to encourage camping and mountaineering; but this would be an official trip, sponsored and actually run by the Sierra Club. The Mazamas, a hiking and camping group founded in 1894 in Oregon, had pioneered large-scale wilderness outings, but those were mainly for pleasure and recreation. The Club's trips, on the other hand, were explicitly aimed at training what we now often call conservation activists.

The first High Trip was held in 1901. Ninety-six people "sauntered," as Muir put it, from the valley to the high country of Yosemite. (He is said to have detested the word "hike," preferring "saunter," which he mistakenly thought was related to *santé*, the French word for health.) The group went via Lake Tenaya and then established a permanent base camp ("Camp Muir") in Tuolumne Meadows, to which provisions had been transported by wagon from Merced. From the meadows, groups of various sizes climbed Mounts Dana, Lyell, and several others, went on fishing expeditions to nearby lakes, and sent an exploring party part way down the Grand Canyon of the Tuolumne.

The *Sierra Club Bulletin* published three different accounts of the trip, one

Joseph N. LeConte. Group posed on the Two Sisters giant sequoia, Kings River Canyon. 1896. Sierra Club Archives

Joseph N. LeConte. Looking across Tuolumne Meadows toward Mount Conner and Mount Dana, with Lembert Dome in center and the Sierra crest in the distance. c. 1895. Sierra Club Archives

OPPOSITE
Joseph N. LeConte. Party at Roaring River Falls on the Kings River. 1896. Sierra Club Archives

Galen Rowell. Sunset after a Storm, Yosemite Valley, California. 1970. Half Dome is visible at center.

by Ella M. Sexton ("A woman's view of the outing"), another by E. T. Parsons ("A man's view of the outing"), and a third by Alexander G. Eells (an account of the excursion down the Tuolumne). All reported a memorable experience, jammed with exciting climbs and hikes and embellished with informative lectures on natural and human history and topical politics. (Parsons went out of his way to exclaim at how strong and good-natured the women were, and Eells closed by warning that for future hikes down the Tuolumne "a man's attire is indispensable to success. Any sort of skirt would make the struggle through the brush simply hopeless.") The campers remained in the high country for nearly three weeks, and returned to the valley and thence to their homes and jobs inspired and refreshed.

The High Trip was born. Two years later a party of 150 clambered to the top of Mount Whitney in what is now Sequoia National Park. Soon groups of as many as three hundred Sierra Clubbers were swarming over their beloved mountains. The High Trip would be an annual affair, with Will Colby as leader until 1930.

The birth of the High Trip was in a sense a rebirth for the Sierra Club. Conservation — the defending of Yosemite and the High Sierra — was a popular enough cause to get the Club off to a strong start, but this was not apparently enough to sustain it during periods when the battle fronts were quiet. The High Trip would build a different kind of organization, based on sharing the wilderness experience with groups of upwards of three hundred people. By the time Colby retired from his volunteer post, there was a strong corps of new members who would move into leadership roles and institute different kinds of trips — for members who liked their crowds a bit smaller, or those who liked to move faster and camp higher than the High Trip could, or those with small children who could not move as far and as often as the High Trips did.

These trips — High Trips, knapsack trips, base camp trips, river trips, and others — would foster a different kind of organization from that of the 1890s: the Club was still devoted to conservation, but it was also involved in wilderness recreation as a major activity. The number of lifelong friendships, business relationships, and romances that began on Sierra Club outings is immeasurable.

❧

RECESSION VERSUS REDUCTION

The perennial effort by economic interests to shrink Yosemite's boundaries came to a head just after the turn of the century. On one side was the Sierra Club, upholding Yosemite's integrity and supporting the "recession" movement, the attempt to wrest control of the valley, its immediate surroundings, and the Mariposa Grove of Big Trees, from the State of California and join it

Joseph N. LeConte. Reflections in Tenaya Lake, Yosemite National Park. 1907. Sierra Club Archives

Cedric Wright. High Trippers returning from an ascent of Mount Ritter, Rodgers Peak at left. 1938. Sierra Club Archives

to the national park. Efforts toward that end, spurred on by damage that the state had permitted to befall the valley, had been mounted since the creation of the national park, but they did not succeed until after President Theodore Roosevelt and California Governor James Pardee visited the valley in 1903, to form their own opinions about the merits of recession. They were accompanied by John Muir and Will Colby, who used the opportunity to make the case for returning the valley to federal control. The governor at one point told Colby that he would sign a recession bill if it could pass the state legislature in Sacramento. Pardee thus tacitly invited the Club to lobby California legislators and acknowledged the nascent political power of its members, collectively and individually. Muir and Colby accepted this invitation and made nine lobbying trips to Sacramento.

On the other side of the "recession" issue, commercial interests were trying to reduce the size of the park by lopping off many townships to the north, east, and west of the valley. Much of the rationale for eliminating land from Yosemite was that it overlay valuable mineral deposits, a topic that occupies the Club's attention to this day.

On February 7, 1905, Congress redrew the park's boundaries, eliminating several townships on the corners of the park and adding a few others. In all, 542 square miles were eliminated and 113 added. It was a defeat for the Sierra Club, which had opposed most of the eliminations and had argued for larger expansion than was finally enacted.

A brighter outcome, however, awaited the recession issue. Will Colby's theory was that California had simply borrowed Yosemite Valley from the United States and that it should now return it, and he, Muir, and others pressed that argument vigorously on lobbying visits to Sacramento. Following loud and rancorous public debate, which filled newspaper pages in San Francisco and other Western cities, the California legislature voted, also in February 1905, to "recede" Yosemite Valley to the care of the federal government. The transfer could not take place, however, until Congress approved it.

Wrangling over recession during the next year and a half allowed the shrink-the-park forces to build up steam for yet another attack, this on behalf of a private railroad company that wanted to build a line from Fresno to the Mariposa Grove and on into the valley. When the recession bill was reintroduced, it was amended by California Senator George Perkins in an attempt to eliminate 24,000 acres on the southwest edge of the park. The Sierra Club strove mightily against this further assault on the park. "There are private railroad, lumber, and cattle interests endeavoring to force an amendment . . . ," Will Colby wrote to Congress, "which would eliminate a large area from the western side of the Yosemite National Park." He went on, "we wish you to be informed that the Sierra Club is unalterably opposed to any change of the present boundaries, and we urge the immediate passage of the bill accepting Yosemite Valley as originally introduced." A counter-amendment that eliminated only half the acreage of Senator Perkins's bill eventually passed.

Thus, in late 1906, Yosemite Valley was returned to the federal government, and added to a park that had been unnecessarily reduced in size.

Edward T. Parsons. Sierra Club members on the summit of Mount Brewer, Kings River Canyon High Trip. 1902. Sierra Club Archives

Edward T. Parsons. Evening at Tuolumne Meadows, ninth annual High Trip to Yosemite and Hetch Hetchy. 1909. Sierra Club Archives

HETCH HETCHY:
JOHN MUIR'S LAST BATTLE

No sooner was ownership of Yosemite National Park consolidated under the federal government than a proposal was put forward to sacrifice Hetch Hetchy Valley, north of Yosemite Valley, for a reservoir for the exclusive benefit of the city of San Francisco. The ensuing struggle would be the biggest yet, both for the Club and for its president, John Muir. It would also be Muir's last.

The San Francisco that had greeted Muir in 1868 was a noisy, bawdy collection of buildings along the eastern shore of the peninsula. The population was several tens of thousands, and there was much bustling to and from the goldfields in the Sierra foothills, though the frenzy of forty-nine was largely past. By the turn of the century San Francisco had become a prosperous city.

Although San Francisco occupies one of the loveliest possible sites for a city, it has several handicaps. One, of course, is the San Andreas and other nearby faults, capable of unleashing calamitous earthquakes with no warning. A serious day-to-day concern is that it is a long way from a reliable supply of fresh water. Several creeks once found their way down the flanks of the city's many hills and flowed eventually into bay or ocean, but they were far from enough to supply the needs of a growing metropolis, and they were pitifully inadequate for emergencies. Fire, for example. Indeed, by 1851, two years into the Gold Rush, when a bucket of fresh water commanded the princely sum of one dollar, San Francisco had burned down six times. During one of the fires, a printing plant burned and released a lava flow of molten lead that streamed all the way to the bay. During another, a desperate businessman saved his building by dousing it with eighty thousand gallons of vinegar. The search for a reliable supply of water would be high on San Franciscans' list of urgent tasks to accomplish.

By the early 1900s, San Francisco politicians and their partisans were quietly beginning a long battle to gain the right to build a reservoir in Hetch Hetchy Valley and a pipeline to transport the water to the city.

John Muir had first visited Hetch Hetchy in 1870. It "is a grand landscape garden, one of nature's rarest and most precious mountain mansions," he wrote later. ("Hetch Hetchy" probably derives from an Ahwahneechee phrase meaning "grassy floor.") "As in Yosemite, the sublime rocks of its walls glow with life, whether leaning back in repose or standing erect in thoughtful attitudes." Indeed, Hetch Hetchy was startlingly similar to Yosemite, "a wonderfully exact counterpart of the Merced Yosemite," as Muir put it, though considerably smaller, with domes and cliffs, waterfalls and glorious meadows. Hetch Hetchy was not as well known as Yosemite; there was no road into it, and the terrain one had to traverse to get there was rough. To those who had seen it, however, Hetch Hetchy was every bit the equal of Yosemite. Many remarked that had it been situated anywhere else, Hetch Hetchy would certainly have been proclaimed a national treasure and natural wonder and preserved for all time.

In 1901 a bill was spirited through Congress so stealthily that no one in the Sierra Club learned of its existence until many months after it became law. It provided authority for the Secretary of the Interior to grant rights-of-way through national parks for roads and pipelines. San Francisco Mayor James Phelan then quietly hired an engineer to study the feasibility of building a reservoir in Hetch Hetchy and several other sites. The report estimated that the dam and reservoir could be constructed for just under $40 million, and that a hydroelectric installation, if built there, could earn enough money to pay for a substantial part of the cost of the dam. Mayor Phelan then filed for reservoir rights at Hetch Hetchy and Lake Eleanor, just to the north of Hetch Hetchy and just within the boundaries of the national park. He did so as an individual, not as mayor, to avoid raising the alarm. Interior Secretary E. A. Hickock denied the application on January 20, 1903, as inappropriate for a national park. Phelan then turned over his prospective interest in the rights application to the City of San Francisco and had his city attorney — Franklin K. Lane, who will later loom large in this story — ask for reconsideration of the permit denial.

The denial was affirmed on December 22, 1903, by Secretary Hickock and reaffirmed on February 20, 1905. A year later, the San Francisco Board of Supervisors voted to abandon all attempts to gain rights to Hetch Hetchy and to pursue other solutions to its water supply problem. But two months later, on April 18, 1906, the city was hit by a violent earthquake, followed by an even more destructive fire. Much of the blame for the damage suffered was laid to the city's inadequate water supply; the supervisors resumed their effort on behalf of Hetch Hetchy.

Following the earthquake and fire the seriousness of the threat to Hetch Hetchy began to emerge.

A principal player in the struggle was a major figure in the history of American conservation, both before the Hetch Hetchy fight and subsequently. His name was Gifford Pinchot and he is frequently spoken of in the same breath with John Muir, as Muir's antithesis in the philosophy of conservation. The differences between what could be called Pinchot's utilitarian views and Muir's esthetic position were brought into focus by the Hetch Hetchy fight.

Pinchot was the first American to be trained as a forester. He had earned degrees in Paris, then returned to the United States and campaigned for the establishment of a federal Forest Service to oversee the vast forest preserves set aside in the 1890s and 1900s. At Pinchot's urging, the Forest Service was set up within the Department of Agriculture, at the beginning of 1905.

Pinchot believed that natural resources existed for the benefit of humanity, that they should be managed scientifically and carefully, and that they should never simply be left alone. His ideal was the manipulation of nature to provide "the greatest good for the greatest number in the long run."

Muir disagreed profoundly. He felt that parts of the natural landscape ought to be left wholly wild, to manage themselves in accordance with

Anon. The Mills Building on Bush Street, San Francisco, after the earthquake and fire of April 18–19, 1906. The headquarters of the Sierra Club moved there in 1903 and was destroyed in the fire but reestablished afterward; it remained in the Mills Building until 1975. California Historical Society, San Francisco

Joseph N. LeConte. View up Sutter Street from Market Street, April 26, 1906, in the aftermath of the great San Francisco earthquake. Sierra Club Archives

OPPOSITE
Joseph N. LeConte. Hetch Hetchy Falls and Valley from across the Tuolumne River. c. 1908. Sierra Club Archives

natural laws. Though Muir and Pinchot started as friends and remained admirers—Pinchot has nothing but high praise for Muir in his autobiography *Breaking New Ground*—they soon grew apart and clashed frequently over matters of public policy.

In addition to his scientific training, Pinchot had great personal charm and powers of persuasion. He was a close friend and advisor to President Theodore Roosevelt, and he is generally credited with changing T. R.'s mind about the wisdom of building the Hetch Hetchy dam and reservoir project. Roosevelt is much admired by conservationists for his strong conservation record, including the preserving of many national monuments and the support of many national parks. Despite his pro-park proclivities, however, Roosevelt eventually came to support the building of the Hetch Hetchy reservoir.[11]

In response to one of San Francisco's several applications for Hetch Hetchy, President Roosevelt had asked his attorney general to give him a legal opinion on whether the city could reopen the matter. Attorney General Purdy said yes, and said also that the Secretary of the Interior could hand the valley over to the city if he wanted to. By this time, Secretary Hickock, who had stood firm against the city, had been replaced by James R. Garfield. Garfield conducted a hearing on the issue on July 27, 1907, and ruled in favor of the city on May 11, 1908.

The Sierra Club, self-appointed defender of Yosemite, was understandably displeased by this ruling, but it was somewhat ambivalent in its response. Muir, Colby, and the others were a bit worn down by the recession campaign, for one thing. For another, there was a vocal minority of members led, ironically, by Warren Olney, in whose office the Club was born—who thought that San Francisco's need for a secure water supply ought to take precedence over the continued existence of a wild Hetch Hetchy and the sanctity of the national park system.

Muir himself, by this time sixty-nine years old, never wavered, and jumped into the battle with his whole being. "This Yosemite fight," he wrote Robert Underwood Johnson in the fall of 1907, "promises to be the worst ever. Try to prevent the Secretary from making sudden decision which our enemies are trying for. Have got the Sierra Club at work. You try to rouse the Appalachian Mountaineering Club. Am writing the President and Garfield." Soon thereafter the Club's board of directors went on record opposing the project and wrote to inform legislators and bureaucrats in Washington of their decision.

This formal opposition to the Hetch Hetchy scheme in turn provoked loud protests from some members of the Club who sided with the city and wrote letters to newspapers and public officials denouncing the action of their leaders. This so discouraged Muir that he offered to resign, not only the presidency but his personal membership as well. Colby talked him out of this notion, saying the entire effort to block the ruination of Hetch Hetchy would collapse without him.

A resolution was introduced in Congress to trade the floor of Hetch Hetchy Valley to San Francisco for land that the city owned in the mountains above. The battle was joined. Pamphlets were prepared using Muir's descriptions of Hetch Hetchy with exhortations to "Let all the People Speak and Prevent the Destruction of the Yosemite National Park." Delegations were dispatched to Washington and testimony was written and delivered. Yosemite was by then famous throughout the country, not least because of Muir's articles and its status as one of the premier national parks. Newspapers in all parts of the country began to cover the story and, in San Francisco at least, to take sides, vociferously. Muir, Colby, Johnson, and their allies prevailed at this stage, with politicians badly split in their positions.

In 1909, the Roosevelt administration gave way to the new presidency of William Howard Taft, like Roosevelt a Republican. Taft replaced Garfield with Richard Ballinger as Secretary of the Interior. Gifford Pinchot remained as head of the Forest Service and thus retained his influence over the fortunes of Hetch Hetchy.

Sierra Club leaders, in close cooperation with their counterparts in the Appalachian Mountain Club, the Mazamas, the Mountaineers of Seattle, and the others, decided to mount a nationwide campaign to persuade Secretary Ballinger to revoke the Garfield permit for construction of a reservoir in Hetch Hetchy. Not only were the widely scattered allies united in their support for a dam-free Hetch Hetchy, they were also interested in defending the integrity of the national park system. If Yosemite could be violated, their own, closer-to-home wildernesses would never be safe.

The ninth annual High Trip was due for the Sierra Club, and Colby decided to spend the final week in Hetch Hetchy, in order to recruit new troops to the preservation cause and to take photographs of the valley for use in the legislative campaign. They invited members of Congress, Secretary Ballinger, and President Taft to join the outing, to see for themselves what San Francisco wanted to drown. Though neither Ballinger nor Taft could participate in the High Trip, the president visited Yosemite and Ballinger toured Hetch Hetchy later in the year.

Colby, Muir, and Edward Parsons produced a pamphlet, signed by Muir, that stated the Sierra Club's argument. This was sent to all members of Congress and spread far and wide to as many influential citizens as could be identified. The San Francisco newspapers, particularly the *Call*, attacked the Club and its campaign, and encouraged dissident members to make a formal break with the Club's leadership. Accordingly, Warren Olney and Marsden Manson demanded a formal poll of Club members to determine if Muir, Colby, and the other pro-Hetch Hetchy directors were actually representing the wishes of the rank and file. (This tradition of direct democracy had guided the Sierra Club since the very first meeting in Olney's office in 1892. Directors were and still are elected by the members on a one-member, one-vote system. The directors then elect their officers from within the board.)

The poll was conducted at the end of January 1910. The two sides wrote and distributed position papers to all members. The arguments will sound familiar to anyone who has participated in a debate about damming a wild river. The pro-dam forces argued that a lake in Hetch Hetchy would be just

Anon. Construction of the O'Shaughnessy Dam and Hetch Hetchy Reservoir on the Tuolumne River in Yosemite National Park. c. 1919. National Park Service

Philip Hyde. Stumps and lifeless sediment line the banks of Hetch Hetchy Reservoir. 1955. Sierra Club Archives

Philip Hyde. O'Shaughnessy Dam and Hetch Hetchy Reservoir. 1955. Sierra Club Archives

OPPOSITE
Philip Hyde. Hetch Hetchy Falls and cliffs from across the reservoir. 1955. Sierra Club Archives. Compare the falls here with the view of them on p. 68, before the dam and reservoir were built.

73

as beautiful as the natural valley, that San Francisco desperately needed a reliable and economical supply of fresh water, and that one Yosemite Valley was enough. The preservationists countered, with great foresight, that visitation to Yosemite was growing so fast that soon the valley would be thronged and that Hetch Hetchy would be in great demand, that there were other sources of water available to San Francisco, and that the national park system must be kept inviolate.

The last argument was paramount. Of what use was the whole idea of national parks "inalienable for all time" if Yosemite could be invaded and violated by the City of San Francisco for its water supply, no matter how urgently needed? How then to refuse an appeal from Denver, say, for a dam

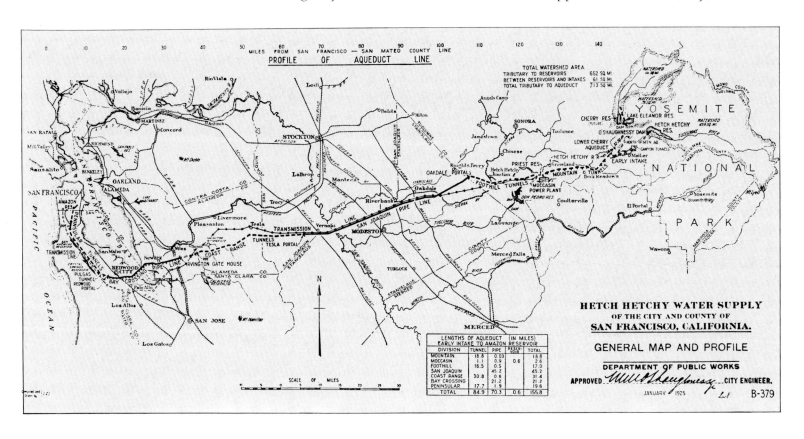

Hetch Hetchy Valley becomes a source of water supply for San Francisco: 1925 map of aqueduct lines signed by William O'Shaughnessy, city engineer. From Ray W. Taylor, *Hetch Hetchy: The Story of San Francisco's Struggle To Provide a Water Supply for Her Future Needs* (San Francisco: Orozco, 1926), opp. 174.

on the Yellowstone River? Or a request from Seattle for a little impoundment on one of the streams flowing down Mount Rainier? It was the abstract as much as the specific that fired passions in this fight, both as thrashed out within the Sierra Club and in Congress and the newspapers. People from across the country expressed their opposition to the sacrifice of a national park to selfish, parochial purposes. Muir wrote in 1911, "These temple destroyers, devotees of ravaging commercialism, seem to have a perfect contempt for Nature, and instead of lifting their eyes to the God of the mountains, lift them to the Almighty Dollar. Dam Hetch Hetchy! As well dam for water-tanks the people's cathedrals and churches, for no holier temple has ever been consecrated by the heart of man."[12]

The argument caught the imagination of most Sierra Club members. When all ballots were counted, the poll stood at 589 in favor of preserving Hetch

Hetchy, 161 in favor of giving it to San Francisco. About fifty members resigned in protest, but the Club could speak with a united voice thereafter.

The period of 1910–12 was one of uncertainty and anxiety for the Sierra Club and its allies. The conservationists were concurrently trying to build and maintain support for their Hetch Hetchy position, to bring pressure on Congress to provide more money for the upkeep, restoration, and development of Yosemite National Park, and to encourage the addition of the Kings Canyon high country to Sequoia National Park.

Hearings about Hetch Hetchy were grueling but inconclusive. In late 1912, just three days before he left office, the Secretary of the Interior, Walter A. Fisher, declared that he lacked statutory authority to issue a permit for the project and that San Francisco should take its request to Congress if it wished to pursue it. San Francisco did.

Woodrow Wilson took office on March 4, 1913, and appointed as Secretary of the Interior Franklin K. Lane—the very man who had, as city attorney of San Francisco, opened the city's campaign for a reservoir in Hetch Hetchy. A more ominous sign for those working to save the valley was hard to imagine.

San Francisco's banner was hoisted by the congressman in whose district Hetch Hetchy lay, one John E. Raker, who introduced a string of five bills between April and August 1913 to grant Hetch Hetchy to San Francisco. The ensuing political contest was surely the most public and prominent conservation battle to that point in American history. Congressional debate filled 380 pages of the *Congressional Record*, a figure few controversies could match. Newspapers across the country took up the issue, with most of the press outside San Francisco firmly in the Sierra Club's camp. Letters and telegrams flooded congressional offices. The Club produced more pamphlets—members' dues supported this activity, along with personal contributions from Muir, Colby, and others—and distributed them to politicians, bureaucrats, editorialists, and other citizens.

In examining the history of this campaign, it is striking how much like subsequent Club battles the fight for Hetch Hetchy actually was. Techniques for publicizing one's point of view have become far more sophisticated and swift, but the general role of publicity was and remains strong and important. Arguments about alternatives to a proposed project still constitute a large part of an overall debate. Political tradeoffs are always in the background, and both sides always claim to have the best interests of the public at heart.

Despite widespread opposition across the country, the House bowed to pressure from San Francisco and its champions and approved Congressman Raker's bill allowing the construction of the dam and reservoir in Hetch Hetchy by the wide margin of 183 to 43. The preservationists would have to make their last stand in the Senate.

The Senate took up the fate of Hetch Hetchy in December and cast its vote at midnight on December 6—San Francisco, 43; Hetch Hetchy, 25. Despite impassioned pleas from the preservationists, Woodrow Wilson signed the bill into law on December 19, 1913.

J. Edward B. Greene. Portrait of John Muir reading, signed by Muir. 1909. Sierra Club Archives

OPPOSITE
Galen Rowell. Split Rock and Cloud, Eastern Sierra, California. 1988. Rowell caught this juxtaposition of cirrus cloud and eighty-foot boulder in the Buttermilk region above Bishop, California, and created an image of formal economy and metaphoric richness.

Hetch Hetchy was lost for a variety of reasons. Pinchot's brand of conservation—stressing "wise development of resources"—prevailed over Muir's vision of the preservation of natural wonders. Sympathy for San Francisco following its destruction by quake and fire was certainly a strong influence. Political amateurs had been outgunned by far more experienced practitioners from San Francisco. Arguments were trotted out that would appear again and again, especially the one that the Sierra Club would keep "progress" at bay in order to defend the selfish interests of its members.

Hetch Hetchy was truly a prototypical political conservation battle for scores more to follow. Hetch Hetchy, the valley, died in 1919 when O'Shaughnessy Dam was completed. Hetch Hetchy, the symbol, would live on.

Muir was deeply saddened by the political defeat but tried to find some consolation. "As to the loss of [Hetch Hetchy] Valley it's hard to bear," he wrote a friend. "The destruction of the charming groves and gardens, the finest in all California, goes to my heart. But in spite of Satan & Co. some sort of compensation must surely come out of this dark damn-dam-damnation."[13]

One year later, on Christmas eve, 1914, suffering from a lung infection, John Muir died at the age of seventy-six. Close associates, including Will Colby, reported that the loss of Hetch Hetchy undoubtedly hastened his death.

His longtime friend and collaborator Robert Underwood Johnson gave one of the many tributes that were written of Muir:

> One almost hesitates to use the word "great" of one who has just passed away, but I believe that history will give a very high place to the indomitable explorer who discovered the great glacier named after him, and whose life for eleven years in the High Sierra resulted in a body of writing of marked excellence, combining accurate and carefully coordinated scientific observation with poetic sensibility and expression. . . . But Muir's public services were not merely scientific and literary. His countrymen owe him gratitude as the pioneer of our system of national parks. Out of the fight which he led for the better care of the Yosemite by the State of California grew the demand for the extension of the system. To this many persons and organizations contributed, but Muir's writings and enthusiasm were the chief forces that inspired the movement. All the other torches were lighted from his.[14]

Anon. Muir, far left, with (clockwise from top) the painter William Keith, Charles Keeler, Francis Brown, and the naturalist John Burroughs. c. 1900. Sierra Club Archives

OPPOSITE
Galen Rowell. Mist over the Merced River, Yosemite Valley, California. 1975

Muir's passing left the Sierra Club without its most inspired visionary, but the battle for Hetch Hetchy had groomed a legion of tough fighters who understood a great deal about how the federal government worked and how public opinion could be enlisted in the pursuit of a political goal. Will Colby, J. N. LeConte (the son of Club cofounder Joseph LeConte), and William F. Badè were three of the most prominent leaders. LeConte was elected Sierra Club president to succeed Muir.

The struggle over Hetch Hetchy had also served to sketch the outlines of many battles to come, battles between beauty and utility, between the philosophies of John Muir and Gifford Pinchot. It had also unified the Club as a result of internal dissent over Hetch Hetchy and the subsequent referendum. It would be some years before there was significant disagreement within the Club over conservation policy.

The fight had also made the name of the Sierra Club known across the country and, though it would be some years before the Club involved itself much in matters outside California and the Pacific Northwest, the public was clearly aware of this band of fighters from California who would battle with vigor and passion to preserve their wild mountains from destruction.

O F
R E C R E A T I O N
A N D
P A R K S

❧

H I K I N G   A N D   S K I I N G   T H E
H I G H   W I L D E R N E S S   A N D
B U I L D I N G   T H E   N A T I O N A L
P A R K   S Y S T E M
1 9 1 5   ❧   1 9 5 0

Galen Rowell. Mount Whitney, Sequoia National Park, California. 1988

OPPOSITE
Galen Rowell. Sierra Crest from the Trail below Mount Whitney, California. 1987. At the end of the John Muir Trail is Mount Whitney. It is an easy stroll to its summit, the highest point in the lower forty-eight states, provided you approach from the west. From the east it is another matter entirely. No one gained the summit that way until August 16, 1931, when the Sierra Club team of Norman Clyde, Jules Eichorn, Glen Dawson, and Robert Underhill — an Englishman who introduced technical rope-climbing to Sierra mountaineers — succeeded in a feat many had thought impossible.

The struggles over Yosemite and Hetch Hetchy were not the only sparks that ignited the burgeoning conservation movement in the late 1800s and early 1900s. The ruthless slaughter of birds for their feathers had inspired formation of the Audubon Society, and the near extirpation of the bison and the razing of Eastern forests had sharpened Americans' sensitivity to the vulnerability of their natural resources, until then considered infinite and inexhaustible. As what had once seemed to be unlimited wilderness slowly dwindled, Americans became more interested in protecting the finest examples of what remained. Thus, the remote and mysterious places of the West — especially Yosemite, Yellowstone, and the Grand Canyon — came to be held in special esteem by people in the East, even though most of them had never seen the places that the historian Wallace Stegner would later call our "geography of hope." Wild places were gaining importance in the public mind. As Stegner wrote, "Something will have gone out of us as a people if we ever let the remaining wilderness be destroyed."

California was by no means immune to this growing concern for wilderness. In 1915, the year after Muir's death, the State of California honored its adopted son by appropriating ten thousand dollars to build a John Muir trail along the Sierra crest from Yosemite Valley to Mount Whitney. This is the heart of Muir's country, encompassing Yosemite and Sequoia National Parks and the soon-to-be-established Kings Canyon National Park. Sierra Club leaders helped in the placement of the route. Completed in the late 1920s, the trail would become a path for pilgrims seeking their own encounters with the places that inspired Muir. It would also be a jumping-off point for many Club outings and excursions, ventures that would continue to build membership and to further the dual mission of enjoying and protecting the moun-

Galen Rowell. Falls on the John Muir
Trail, Yosemite National Park,
California. 1990

LEFT
Galen Rowell. Skiing on the John Muir
Trail, California. 1988

Cedric Wright. Mount Clarence King and its reflection, Kearsarge Pass region, Kings Canyon National Park. c. 1940. Sierra Club Archives

Herbert W. Gleason. Paradise Park, July 1905. Sierra Club excursion up Mount Rainier, Washington. Herbert W. Gleason Collection, Boston

Cedric Wright. A packer beside Muir Hut, Muir Pass, Kings Canyon National Park. c. 1950. Sierra Club Archives

Cedric Wright. The John Muir Trail in Kings Canyon National Park, on the way to Muir Pass. c. 1946. Sierra Club Archives

Edward T. Parsons. On the second Sierra Club High Trip, a group crosses a snowfield on the way to climb Mount Brewer, Kings River Canyon. 1902. Sierra Club Archives

Edward T. Parsons. Supper at base camp near timberline, Tyndall Creek Valley, during the third annual High Trip, Kern River Canyon. 1903. Sierra Club Archives

Joseph N. LeConte. Sierra Club members pose for a photographer at Farewell Gap, Kern River High Trip. 1903. Sierra Club Archives. A gifted photographer and avid mountaineer, LeConte served as the second president of the Sierra Club, elected after John Muir died in 1914. His father, Joseph LeConte, a professor of geology at the University of California and a Club founder, is portrayed on p. 48.

Edward T. Parsons. Campfire on Moraine Lake during a High Trip to Kings River Canyon. 1908. Sierra Club Archives

Edward T. Parsons. On the summit of Mount Brewer, Kings River Canyon High Trip, 1902. Women participated in the earliest High Trips and pants and high boots were a practical uniform. The Club's first woman president, Aurelia Harwood, served in 1927–28, and was a mountain climber, like virtually all Club leaders.

tains. High Trips and mountain climbs were also the training ground for a new generation of leaders, wilderness lovers who would carry the Club into the second half of the twentieth century and into resource battles undreamed of in John Muir's day.

On the heels of the establishment of the John Muir Trail came another event that would serve to validate Muir's philosophy: the creation in 1916 of the National Park Service, a federal agency to oversee and protect the national parks. This was the achievement of conservationists across the country—all the Hetch Hetchy allies supported the cause—and the Club enlisted immediately in favor of the new agency and its mission. In the next few decades it worked in close cooperation with the agency in building the national park system.

So the Club advanced on two fronts. As its outings flourished and introduced new legions to the joys of the out-of-doors, its leaders were cooperating with politicians and bureaucrats to defend existing protected areas and set aside new ones. And, when they weren't dickering with bureaucrats and persuading politicians, they might well be out bagging peaks and inventing new techniques for conquering unclimbable rock faces. And, when all that was done, they would be starting to publish books about their beloved mountains, the beginning of a long and distinguished publishing tradition.

"CLIMB THE MOUNTAINS AND GET THEIR GOOD TIDINGS"

John Muir's advice has always been followed punctiliously by his organization, right from the first High Trip in 1901. The early outings he encouraged were not altogether primitive. Each High Tripper was permitted to bring a dunnage bag containing as much as forty pounds. (Several reports say that it was a matter of pride among participants to bring precisely forty pounds—no more, surely, but also no less.) This poundage would generally consist of sleeping bag, ground cover, tarp or tent, air mattress, extra footwear, clothes, toiletries, and so forth. Optional accessories included musical instruments, cameras, binoculars, insect repellent, fishing equipment, and practical and recreational books and beverages. The dunnage was consigned to mules, which also packed in the kitchen—stoves, cook pots, frying pans, grates, and more tarps to keep off the almost inevitable afternoon thundershowers. Cooking and pot washing were the responsibility of the staff, generally one professional cook and a slew of college students who made up the commissary. Camps were generally laid out with single men clustered at one end, single women at the other, and married couples in between.

Camp would usually move once in three or four days, something like ten miles at a clip. Between moves there was ample time for mountain climbing, fishing, photography, reading, and administering to sunburn and blisters.

Annual *Bulletins* published accounts of the previous year's High Trip. The following, written by the then-little-known photographer Ansel Adams, is fairly typical of such reports. The excerpts shed light not only on the young artist and mountaineer, but also in a general way on the kind of people who belonged to the Club, those sportsmen-turned-activists whose philosophy followed upon their pleasure.

> The days are replete with adventure; the morning of the first tribal trek is memorable always. You feel a part of an important emigration; there is discipline and precision, but never of military quality. Camp is deftly broken, breakfast consumed, and the day is before you in a blare of light and enthusiasm. . . .
>
> Mid-afternoon . . . a brisk wind breathed silver on the willows bordering the Tuolumne and hustled some scattered clouds beyond Kuna Crest. It was the first day of the outing—you were a little tired and dusty, but quite excited in spite of yourself. You were already aware that contact with fundamental earthy things gave a startling perspective on the high-spun realities of modern life. No matter how sophisticate[d] you may be, a huge granite mountain cannot be denied—it speaks in silence to the very core of your being. . . .
>
> The first dinner in camp is a great occasion, especially for the initiates, who receive illustrated instruction in the ethics of our primitive cafeteria. It is then you get your spoon, a sort of *visa* to all subsequent meals. If you lose it, you are in for diplomatic difficulties of no mean degree. The spoon is the insignia of the order; without it you are disfranchised and helpless. It usually reposes between the sock and boot-top, but some are drilled and hang on the bearers' bosoms like medals. Literally, you are born into the Sierra Club with a steel spoon in your mouth.

Camp fire was one of the important events of the High Trip. Elaborate skits were written and presented, excellent concerts were performed on fiddle and recorder, eloquent speeches were delivered on conservation struggles of the day, and many voices were raised in enthusiastic harmony.

In addition to the camaraderie of the campsite, Adams describes the Sierra itself—its details as well as its heart-stopping vistas.

> The trail from Neall and Rodgers lakes to Benson Lake presents a new order of beauty. . . . Our camp near Benson Lake was set in a refreshing jungle of lodgepole pine and willow, with a study support of red fir. It was distributed over several little islands, interconnected by logs—a thoroughly woodsy environment with immense entrancing detail. Millions upon millions of friendly living things crowd the soil, the edges of pools, the spaces under the leaves, and in the sunny openings of the forest. A hushed and swiftly moving life enters your consciousness as myriad sparklings of light and color and the frail sounds of faery wings. Glorious dragon-flies move as bolts of blue

Joseph N. LeConte. Fourth of July dinner in the Sierra Club High Trip camp on the Kern River. 1903. Sierra Club Archives

George R. King. Signor De Grassi entertains in camp at Tuolumne Meadows, 1909 High Trip. Sierra Club Archives

Edward T. Parsons. Couples dance the Flora Dora, second High Trip, Kings River Canyon. 1902. Sierra Club Archives

Joseph N. LeConte. Marian Randall Parsons, a Club director from 1914 to 1938, and friends in a humorous tableau they called "Sack-o-Germea" (punning on the names of the Indian guide Sacajawea and a breakfast cereal of the day), Mount Rainier High Trip. 1905. Sierra Club Archives

Joseph N. LeConte. Group of hungry Sierrans in camp at Mineral King Valley. 1903. Sierra Club Archives

lightning over the waters; mysterious larvae propel their grotesque courses through the shallows. Iridescent clouds of gnats pulsate in the sun, bees hang on swaying blossoms, and small earthy creatures concern themselves with their problems of existence. . . .

[At Garnet Lake, east of Yosemite] we were favored with vigorous days of storm that augmented the severe grandeur of the peaks; sky and mountains were unified in patterns of dynamic splendor. [On the morning of the day we climbed Mount Ritter] the sky was thronged with cloud and a sharp wind beat upon the crags. Before noon an eager arm of cloud clutched at the sun, and a sigh of shadow came over the mountains. Rippling patterns of wind flashed on turquoise waters — ice-fields became cold gray as the moon before dawn. It was good to feel the tiny flagellations of the rain — it was good to be buffeted by cool and fragrant air. And one must ever bow before the deep benediction of thunder. . . .[15]

Thus Adams recounted the High Trip of 1931. Other accounts are similar. For all the blisters and mosquito bites, for all the sunburn and thunderstorms, the overpowering influence of the mountains swept people up, bringing them back on outings year after year and motivating many to undertake active volunteer service in the cause of conservation.

By the thirties, mountaineering and rock climbing dominated the Club's activities. They also led to a close camaraderie among participants and became the training-ground for a group of youths who would lead the Club into its second half-century.

The center of the Club's rock-climbing activity — away from the mountains themselves, that is — was a large, cracked, pitted boulder lodged halfway up the Berkeley hills outside San Francisco and known as Cragmont Rock. To

Ansel Adams. "The Management Watches." High Trip members in camp at Benson Lake. 1931. © 1991 Trustees of the Ansel Adams Publishing Rights Trust. Adams inscribed this work and "The Kitchen Police" (below, opposite), and other droll vignettes in the albums he made of the photographs he took on years of High Trips. Following the trips the albums could be viewed at the Club and Adams made prints to order from them. The albums continue to reside in the Sierra Club Archives.

Ansel Adams. Sierra Club cups, a photograph Adams paired with that of the eggs in a nest (above, opposite) in his album of the 1933 High Trip to the Evolution and Palisades regions. © 1991 Trustees of the Ansel Adams Publishing Rights Trust

Cedric Wright. Camp at Garnet Lake,
1938 High Trip. Sierra Club Archives

Anon. "Holding the Life Line" for a climber ascending a canyon wall, Rainbow Bridge National Monument, Utah, 1925 album in Sierra Club Archives

Anon. Rainbow Bridge National Monument, Utah, 1925 album in Sierra Club Archives

Ansel Adams. Sierra Club pack train crossing Elizabeth Pass, Mount Whitney region, 1932 High Trip. © 1991 Trustees of the Ansel Adams Publishing Rights Trust

Joseph N. LeConte. A friend identified only as "Jim" on the summit of Mount Brewer, Kings River Canyon. 1895. Sierra Club Archives

Joseph N. LeConte. Panorama of the Kings River watershed looking south from Mount Gardner. 1896. Sierra Club Archives

this day climbers hang by their fingertips from the ledges on Cragmont Rock. In the 1930s too, climbers hung there, often under the watchful eye of Dick Leonard.

Leonard lived in Berkeley and practiced law in San Francisco. He had first visited the Sierra — the Kings Canyon backcountry — in 1930 and had become interested in mountaineering and rock climbing. His legal studies precluded frequent trips to the mountains to slake his thirst for granite, however, so Leonard organized a group of budding climbers to hone their skills closer to home. They became interested in technical climbing: the use of direct aids like ropes, pitons (spikes with holes at one end for ropes), and the oversized, safety pin-like devices known as carabiners. Europeans had developed the use of such gear, partly because of the many glaciers that exist in the Alps and the necessity of using ropes, crampons, and ice axes to avoid the dangers of tumbling into icy crevasses. The Sierra, on the contrary, has only tiny remnant glaciers, which can be easily avoided in virtually all circumstances. Until Leonard's day, Sierra climbers would rope themselves together when crossing steep snowfields, but they seldom used ropes on rock.

A visit by the British mountaineer Robert Underhill to the 1931 High Trip helped change that, indeed to change American rock climbing for all time. At Leonard's request, Underhill demonstrated "direct aid" to members — how by driving pitons into cracks too shallow for finger-holds, then clipping a carabiner-held rope into the piton's hole, climbers could scale sheer faces that previous climbers could only yearn for. There was still considerable danger, of course. Climbing, the leader would still be above his last piton as he drove in the next, and if he fell, he would either suffer a nasty and dangerous jolt when brought up short by the piton-held rope, or, worse, the piton could pull out or the rope could break. To overcome this problem, Leonard devised what he called the "dynamic belay," in which the leader's rope would be secured around the waist of a companion safely wedged into secure rocks or braced by still more pitons. Then if the leader fell, the belayer could pay out enough slack to cushion the fall. Climbing techniques and safety measures learned and sharpened on Cragmont Rock would lead to ascents of previously unconquerable rock faces in Yosemite Valley, Kings Canyon, and scores of other spectacular places.

Here is a sample of what Leonard reported, with typical lawyerly precision, in "Rock-Climbing in the Yosemite Region" in the 1936 annual *Bulletin*. The objective was one of the best-known features of Yosemite Valley, a challenge to climbers ever since people began hoisting themselves up Sierra granite for the pure joy of doing so. Though it now has fixed cables to make the climb fairly easy, in the early days it was one of the most difficult ascents known.

> *Half Dome.* — In June 1933, Henry S. Beers, Bestor Robinson, and I conceived the plan of attempting to climb the rounded face on the Glacier Point side. Without pitons, we were stopped at a point only 300 feet from the base by almost holdless granite at an angle of 65 degrees. We returned to the valley by an interesting route from the Diving Board to the base of the face of Half Dome, thence down to

Cedric Wright. Sierra Club climbers approach the summit of Mount Resplendent in the Canadian Rockies, 1928 High Trip. Sierra Club Archives

BELOW RIGHT
Cedric Wright. Norman Clyde, who taught the art of mountaineering to a generation of Sierra Club enthusiasts, during a High Trip. c. 1938. Sierra Club Archives

BELOW
David R. Brower. Hervey Voge on Pinnacle Rock, one of several rock-climbing practice sites in Berkeley. 1934. Collection of David Brower

John Dyer. The Sierra Club party that made the first ascent of Shiprock, New Mexico, crosses below its east face, October 8, 1939. Collection of David Brower

Anon. Club members Allen DeWitt, Torcom Bedayan, and Robin Hansen made the first ascent in 1940 of Kat Pinnacle, a spectacular formation in Yosemite Valley. Sierra Club Archives

Cedric Wright. Norman Clyde's battered, *tricouni*-nailed climbing boots. 1950s. Sierra Club Archives

OPPOSITE
Galen Rowell. Ron Kauk Free-Soloing next to Yosemite Falls (with Half Dome in the Background), Yosemite Valley, California. 1987. Rock climbing can be very moralistic. Climbers endlessly debate the ethics of one technique over another, on and off season, in camp and in the pages of such climbers' magazines as the Sierra Club's *Ascent.* Is it acceptable to pound pitons into granite cracks? If so, can they be left there for the next party or must one remove them? Do pitons do unacceptable damage to the rock face? Demean the sport? Violate the dignity of the mountain? The climber here, Ron Kauk, photographed by Galen Rowell, a world-class climber himself, exemplifies a trend away from mechanical aids of any kind in climbing, including ropes. His sport is definitely not for the faint-of-heart.

Mirror Lake. Two years later I tried it again with David R. Brower and Jules M. Eichorn. In spite of the fact that we had complete piton equipment we were able to climb only 75 feet higher than on the former attempt. We spent four hours sitting, two at a time, on a three-inch tree, while the third attempted to work out a possible route. Although caught by darkness halfway down, due to the prolonged climbing attack, we were duly prepared with emergency equipment and had no trouble in completing the remaining 1,500 feet of roped climbing with the aid of our lights. On September 8, 1935, Brower, Robinson, and I tried the climb for the third and, for us, the last time. With an early start, we followed LeConte's route up the gully near Grizzly Peak and reached the plateau between it and Half Dome at 8 A.M. There we were stopped nearly 1,000 feet below our previous highest point by a view of the face that convinced us that it could not be climbed without excessive use of pitons as artificial aid. The undefined borderline between justifiable and unjustifiable use of direct aid would have to be crossed. . . .

Ah, the undefined borderline. How many pitons is too many pitons? Is it ethical to drive spikes all the way up the face of a mountain in order to haul yourself up hand-over-hand, with the rope clamps called jumars? What about drills and expansion bolts? Is it disrespectful to the mountains to use such gear? These questions were debated at great length as the years went by.

Cathedral Rocks. — These were climbed as early as October 1864 by Clarence King [one of the first to climb extensively in and around Yosemite], using a route down Bridalveil Creek. The more interesting [anyone else would probably call it "terrifying"] route up the lower gully has been climbed several times by Charles and Enid Michael. . . . On May 27, 1934, Doris Corcoran (now Mrs. Leonard) and I attempted the NW face of the lower Cathedral Rock. Our reconnaissance to a height of 1,000 feet in a driving rain convinced us that the overhangs of the upper portion would be very difficult. On September 7, 1935, Bestor Robinson, Doris Leonard, and I made the first ascent of this face. The problem consists in working out from under a massive overhang on a 70-degree face 1,100 feet above the valley floor. Due to lack of holds at this point, three pitons were used as direct aids with seven others for safety. A six-foot fall of the leader from twenty feet above was easily held by the belayer standing on two pitons on the 70-degree face, and anchored through two other pitons by Doris sixty feet below. Although the difficult portion is only 150 feet high, the piton technique is as intricate as anything yet accomplished by our group.[16]

Though the Sierra was the site of most of the Club's climbing and camping, there were excursions to other ranges, to other challenges, as well. One of the most famous in climbing circles took a team of five to the Southwest.

Ansel Adams. Roping down, 1933 High Trip. © 1991 Trustees of the Ansel Adams Publishing Rights Trust

In northern New Mexico stands the core of an old volcano known as Shiprock, riding the dry waves of sand and sandstone that spread from its base in all directions. Until four Sierra Club climbers set out in October 1939, Shiprock — soaring 1,700 feet above the desert — had rebuffed all attempts to attain the crow's nest and had nearly killed at least one climber making the attempt.

The four were Raffi Bedayn, Bestor Robinson, John Dyer, and David Brower, with Dick Leonard in a nonclimbing supporting role. Climbing was treacherous in the friable material of Shiprock, and they had to inch their way upwards for a day, then as they ran out of daylight, retreat and try again. For two days they made slow, difficult progress, then returned to the desert floor. Their route, had anyone painted it on the side of the mountain, would look like a comic-book lightning storm. They used pitons, ropes, carabiners, and a new invention, the expansion bolt. At the midpoint of the fourth day (they spent the third night in a cave high up on the Rock), they gained the summit. It took three and a half days to make the ascent; then half a day to collect their hardware and return to solid ground. Until the Navajos declared the peak — along with many other sacred mountains on the reservation — off limits in 1970, Shiprock would be a mecca for serious climbers.[17]

Rock climbing itself would prove to be a rite of passage for Club members. People who depended so basically on each other's strength, nerve, skill, and good judgment would likely become strong friends and devoted spouses, and so it turned out. In addition, the relationships tied together with climbing ropes carried over to leadership posts in the Sierra Club.

In his 1936 report Leonard mentioned two men who would become prominent in the Club, Bestor Robinson and David Brower. Robinson was, like Leonard, an attorney and an avid outdoorsman, mountaineer, and rock climber. He was active in club affairs for a half century, serving for the normal one-year terms as president. Other names crop up in Dick Leonard's 1936 report: Jules Eichorn, Hervey Voge, Morgan Harris, Peter Grubb, Raffi Bedayn — all of whom helped shape the personality of the organization between the World Wars and afterward. Of them, David Brower left the most distinctive footprint.

DAVID BROWER: THE EDUCATION OF AN ARCHDRUID

A native of Berkeley, the young Dave Brower was tall, lanky, and painfully shy. He was given to solitary rambles in the then-wild hills above the town, and he developed a gift for description of the natural scene by painting word pictures for his blind mother. At age six, he had been introduced to the Sierra by his engineer father and, like Muir, Leonard, and Ansel Adams, he was drawn eventually to Yosemite.

Cedric Wright. Ansel Adams with his camera perched atop his car and aimed toward the Owens Valley, Mount Williamson in the background. c. 1946. Sierra Club Archives

Perhaps one of the best-loved twentieth-century American photographers, Ansel Adams was also a host, a storyteller of legendary reputation, and a pianist of professional quality, able to perform in the customary fashion, with his fingers, and also with oranges—and even on occasion with his own backside. He was a photography teacher of skill and dedication who led generations of students on field trips to Yosemite.

Brower took his first steps toward a lifelong association with the Sierra Club via a chance meeting with Hervey Voge in the high country near the Palisades in 1933. Upon hearing Brower's accounts of several daredevil climbs, Voge suggested that Brower try the rock-climbing sessions that the Sierra Club was sponsoring in and around the Bay Area, particularly at Cragmont Rock, and learn some basic safety techniques. Brower did so, and met other young climbers who were to become Club leaders, including Leonard and Robinson. They sharpened their skills and plotted new routes up the Sierra peaks.

In those days one could not become a member of the Sierra Club by mail. An applicant for membership had to be sponsored by two members in good standing. This provision assured that members belonged because they really wanted to belong and meant that people seldom abandoned their Club memberships.

Leonard and Voge became Brower's sponsors, and three months later, he joined the Sierra Club. The day after his encounter with Voge in the mountains, Brower had run into "this bearded type, camera and tripod over his shoulder, coming up through the timberline forest." It was Ansel Adams, whose photographs Brower had admired in the *Bulletin*. Brower and Adams would become fast friends and frequent collaborators.

By 1935 Brower had contributed his first article to the *Bulletin*; soon he joined the magazine's editorial board and by 1941 had been elected to the board of directors.

In the mid-thirties, Brower worked as publicist for the Yosemite Park and Curry Company, a private concern that operated the hotels and restaurants in the park. (When Congress established the National Park Service, it decreed

112

that the agency could issue leases to private concerns to provide food, lodging, and minimal recreation services to the public at a price to be regulated by the government. It is a system that still prevails in most national parks and monuments, though it is not without its detractors.)

Brower recalls that he enjoyed the job largely because he was able to work intimately with Adams (also on the company payroll) and make extensive use of Adams's photographs. Brower studied photography at the master's knee and turned his skill toward photographing visiting celebrities posed in front of Half Dome, then sending the picture to the subject's home-town newspaper with a press release about what a grand time the visitor was having in Yosemite. Looking back, he is somewhat ambivalent about having worked for the Curry Company. "Ansel's pictures were likewise used," Brower writes in his autobiography, "by the Advertising Department so that it could entice more people to come to Yosemite and overcrowd it."[18]

The two men shared many trips into the Sierra wilderness and insights into what was important about the world and about life. Their collaboration would lead first to Brower's eventual appointment as the Club's first executive director in 1952 and later to the Club's plunge into large-scale commercial publishing of fine books of photography.

Adams was already a relative old-timer, having joined the Club in 1919. A native of San Francisco, he was a talented musician, who then also dabbled in photography. Born in 1902, he had first visited Yosemite at the age of fourteen and had been, like Muir, captivated by the place. As a young man Adams spent more and more of his time there, increasingly with his camera, and by 1919 had taken a job as caretaker of the Club's LeConte Lodge in the Valley. By the late twenties he was a professional photographer making

Ansel Adams was a tireless conservationist both officially — as a director of the Sierra Club from 1934 to 1971 — and as a private citizen. So persistent were his efforts to have Interior Secretary James Watt removed and so lofty his reputation that he was invited by President Reagan to the White House to discuss his ecological concerns. Afterward he told a national magazine: "They are people who know the price of everything. And the value of nothing." When Adams died in 1984 he was working on a "Manifesto for Earth" to combat the Reagan administration's environmental policies.

From posters to produce labels, early advertisers capitalized on the attractions of Yosemite — first as a summer holiday destination and by the beginning of the century as a site for winter sports, lengthening the normal travel season. The Southern Pacific Railroad brochure cover, c. 1910 (opposite left), dramatizes Half Dome and Glacier Point like Fiske's photograph of these landmarks of c. 1880 on p. 11. Courtesy Yosemite National Park Research Library. Photos: Woolard Graphic Service

David R. Brower. Brower's sons Robert and Kenneth on a 1960 ski mountaineering trip, in camp at Donner Summit in the Sierra (Donner Lake below in the distance). Collection of David Brower

Anon. Clair Tappaan Lodge, built in 1934 and named for a former Club president, director, and outings program manager, is the Sierra Club's ski cabin near Donner Summit in the Sierra Nevada. Several generations of members have enjoyed its rustic comforts in winter and summer. c. 1938. Sierra Club Archives

OPPOSITE
Ed Cooper. Climbers traverse a snowfield in the North Cascades Primitive Area, Washington. 1960s. Sierra Club Archives

pictures for the Yosemite Park and Curry Company, pictures that have since become classics of American nature photography. Adams contributed a portfolio to the 1931 *Bulletin*, and in 1934 he began a thirty-seven-year stint on the board of directors.

❧

HICKORY WINGS

It is one thing to hike, camp, and climb in the summer when temperatures are usually mild and precipitation is infrequent and generally liquid. It is something else again to venture into the high country in winter. It is more hazardous; there is less room for error. But it has its clear and compelling advantages, particularly if one likes solitude. A trip on skis into remote Sierra valleys in what is unfairly called the dead of winter is almost certain to be a very private affair. Those who partake of the sport, as many in the Sierra Club did and do, tend to be passionate devotees.

There is also the sport of alpine, or downhill, skiing, which, since it began to gain popularity in the 1930s, has become the dominant winter recreation in mountains throughout the world. This involves mechanical lifts of various designs that transport skiers to the tops of snowy slopes whence they slide down. This offers the opportunity for competition, skiers racing either against each other or against the clock. By the 1930s both kinds of skiing had caught on with Sierra Club members and with their organization. The *Bulletin* began to publish stories and picture essays on skiing, principally ski touring (what is now commonly referred to as cross-country skiing) and ski mountaineering.

The growing popularity of skiing brought suggestions that the Club provide cabins along popular ski-touring routes, since not everyone was interested in the rigorous activity of camping out in the snow. European climbers and hikers had built cabins throughout the Alps, where they could sleep, eat, and take refuge from the weather throughout the year. In New England, where weather can be violent and dangerous, there are some huts, but Western outdoorsmen disdained such development, preferring to leave their mountains as purely wild as possible, believing with Muir that sleeping on the ground and getting the occasional drop of rain in the face was an important part of the wilderness experience.

Winter travel would inspire a few exceptions to the rule, however, and the Club soon found itself landlord of a string of modest ski accommodations, the largest of which is Clair Tappaan Lodge, completed in 1934 near Donner Pass. Other, smaller cabins were built near Clair Tappaan, a day's skiing apart from each other. Another cluster was erected in Southern California, again for skiers. Skiing was, and remains, a principal activity of the Club, and disputes over how and whether to expand facilities for skiing would get the organization into a few quarrels in the coming years.

M. Frank Strauss. The 1903 dedication ceremony for the LeConte Memorial Lodge in Yosemite Valley, built to honor geologist and Sierra Club founder Joseph LeConte. The building, a National Historic Landmark, is still in use as a library and interpretive historic site. Sierra Club Archives

❧

THE RISE OF THE NATIONAL PARK SERVICE

As noted earlier, a half century after the creation of the Yosemite reserve, Congress established an agency to be exclusively responsible for management of the national parks. Until that time there had not been enough parks to warrant such attention, and visitation to the parks was small enough that a large cadre of rangers was not needed. By the early twentieth century, however, the parks were becoming popular, and it was evident that an agency was needed to oversee the development of the parks and to regulate services — hotels, restaurants, and the like — that were provided to the visitors. A federal agency with responsibility for all the national parks seemed the obvious answer.

Such a course had been urged on the government by conservationists and their organizations, the Sierra Club, the Appalachian Mountain Club, and all the rest, as a way to ensure that the national parks received their due recognition and thus the protection they would need from the various types of destroyers that would be forever hankering after their treasures. In 1916, three years after the climax of the Hetch Hetchy battle, Congress created the National Park Service.

The first director of the National Park Service, and the man largely responsible for its development, was Stephen Mather, a member of the Sierra Club who had been an outspoken opponent of the Hetch Hetchy reservoir. Mather, a native of San Francisco, had joined the Club in 1904. He had attended the University of California, spent five years as a newspaper reporter, then become wealthy in the borax business. As his longtime deputy, Horace Albright, wrote later, "There is no doubt he was one of the great salesmen of his time." When, in 1914, following the conclusion of the Hetch Hetchy conflict, Mather took a trip into the backcountry of Sequoia National Park, he was appalled at the neglect and mismanagement he found. He complained to Interior Secretary Franklin K. Lane, an old college friend. Lane replied, "Dear Steve, If you don't like the way the national parks are being run, come on down to Washington and run them yourself." Mather did. He would apply all his powers of salesmanship—and not a little of his personal wealth—to building public support for the national parks and for the creation of the National Park Service in 1916.

Secretary Lane had been one of the principal villains of the Hetch Hetchy saga, but once he had secured the place for San Francisco, Lane had become quite the conservationist. Now he joined forces with Horace Albright to draft principles for administration of the national parks that were strongly preservationist. (Had the Lane/Albright principles been in place in 1913, the Hetch Hetchy reservoir would never have been built.)

The Park Service and the Sierra Club worked more closely during this period than any other. Mather was in constant contact with the Club, seeking advice and support for new park proposals. Together, Mather, Albright, and Club leaders held off most requests for permission to graze livestock in the parks. By 1917, the majority of the employees of the Park Service were Californians with strong ties to the Club. An important link was forged when a young Club member named Francis Farquhar went to Washington in 1918 as part of his Navy duty in World War I. After his discharge from the service, Farquhar would work for the Park Service, later returning to California and serving for twenty years as editor of the *Bulletin*.

In 1919, Mather and Farquhar toured the country, singing the praises of the parks and squiring politicians and influential citizens to places they deemed worthy of designation as national parks. They worked closely with Club leaders both to expand the size of Sequoia National Park—the old dream of Muir's—and to fend off water-rights applications by the City of Los Angeles for several streams in Yosemite and Kings Canyon.

As the close cooperation described above suggests, the 1920s saw a shift in the dynamics of conservation policy-making in the country. Before World War I, the real leaders in conservation—John Muir, Will Colby, and Horace

Ansel Adams. Stephen Mather, an early Club leader and the first director of the National Park Service, at the dedication ceremony for the expanded Sequoia National Park in 1926. © 1991 Trustees of the Ansel Adams Publishing Rights Trust

120

McFarland, among them—had been outside government. (The one exception to this rule was Gifford Pinchot.) Muir and Robert Underwood Johnson had inspired the creation of Yosemite and Sequoia National Parks, while other citizen conservationists had led in the creation of Mount Rainier and Grand Canyon National Parks in the late nineties. But with the passing of Muir in 1914 and the appointment of Mather to the National Park Service in 1916, the Club found itself working more and more in cooperation with government employees to fashion policy, promote new parks, expand existing ones, and fend off attacks from economic interests. Initiative for the establishment of new parks and other protected areas had passed to leaders in Washington, D.C.—supported vigorously, of course, by private citizens. Club historian Michael Cohen describes it bluntly: "Through the 1920s the Club was completely engaged in supporting and supplementing the policy of the Park Service."[19]

Anon. Francis H. Farquhar completes the first ascent of Middle Palisade in 1921. A noted mountaineer and Club president in 1933–35 and 1948–49, he helped introduce advanced rope technique to Sierra climbers. He also established one of the early close links between the Club and the National Park Service, and he later served for nearly twenty years as editor of the *Sierra Club Bulletin.* Sierra Club Archives

BREAKING NEW GROUND

One of the Sierra Club's official purposes, adopted in 1892, was "to publish authentic information" about the mountain regions of the Pacific Coast. To that end, the *Bulletin* had begun publication in 1893, and it was joined by occasional maps and scientific papers. The Club's first book, not counting collections reprinted from the *Bulletin,* was Francis Farquhar's *Place Names of the High Sierra,* published in 1926. As Farquhar reports in his introduction, Club climbers and campers had spent hours upon hours in futile speculation around hundreds of campfires, trying to guess how their favorite peaks, valleys, streams, and meadows had come by their names. Farquhar decided to find out, and to publish his findings. He combed what literature he could unearth and interviewed likely sources of information. He published articles in three annual *Bulletins* (1923–25), and those articles, along with the advice, corrections, and suggestions he received from Club members, were then turned into a book.

Place Names was soon followed by *Starr's Guide to the John Muir Trail* by Walter A. Starr, Jr., a bittersweet story in itself. Starr was a brilliant young lawyer (he had completed the undergraduate and law school course at Stanford in five years), the son of a Club stalwart who would later serve two years as president, and a devoted mountaineer. To celebrate the completion of the John Muir Trail, young Starr set out to write a comprehensive guide to the trail and to the various laterals and spurs that take the hiker on beautiful tangents. Till today the book has been kept available through twelve printings, and it is updated every few years to accommodate the changes—in the availability of firewood, the condition of the trail, the likelihood of crowding, and so on—that have taken place since previous editions. Sad to say, Starr did not live to see even the first edition of his *Guide* in print: he

Carr Clifton. Tufa Formations and the Sierra Crest, Mono Lake, California. 1983. Tufa is a porous rock formed as a deposit from springs or streams. These bizarre forms hint at the geothermal activity in this area, where small earthquakes are frequent, and indicate that this field—and the Mono Lake region—was under water eons ago. For another view of Mono Lake, see pp. 250–51.

fell to his death while climbing in the Sierra Minarets in 1930 at the age of twenty-seven.

Third of the Club's books was *A Journal of Ramblings Through the High Sierra of California* by Joseph LeConte (*père*; his son, J. N. LeConte, succeeded Muir as the Club's president in 1915). LeConte senior was a geologist, a cofounder of the Club, and an accomplished photographer, whose record of the pre-dam Hetch Hetchy Valley is the most thorough and beautiful that exists. The *Journal* was the book version of a report issued by LeConte following an exploratory trip taken by a group from the University of California in 1870. Shorter versions had appeared in *Bulletins* in the early part of the century. The book was published to satisfy the growing interest that Club members and the public were exhibiting in the mountains in the 1930s. All three books carried on the tradition of encouraging people to visit and come to know and appreciate the mountains. If those people would join the Sierra Club and its crusade to protect and preserve those same mountains, so much the better.

The Club continued its geographical spread during this period as well. As noted before, the Southern California (later renamed Angeles) Chapter was established in Los Angeles in 1911, in part to help in the Hetch Hetchy fight. The San Francisco Bay Chapter came into being in 1924, for both recreation and conservation purposes. The Riverside Chapter (California) was created in 1932 and the Loma Prieta Chapter (also California) in 1933, again with active outings programs, some with rock-climbing sections. These local chapters began climbing mountains and putting names on many of the unnamed peaks and lakes in the remote Sierra wilderness. Such local chapters, tied together by outings and other social events and allied with other chapters and the national organization by virtue of their interest in matters of national conservation policy, were to give the Sierra Club its unique identity. Other local recreation groups existed and continue to exist today, of course, and national groups concerned with natural resource protection, conservation politics, and environmental policy exist as well. But none blends the two in quite the way the Sierra Club did and does, in a two-way street where the national organization provides support for chapter functions, and the chapters drum up support for national campaigns.

❧

KINGS CANYON NATIONAL PARK

In the thirties, as chapters multiplied in California, members mobilized to establish another major park in the Sierra south of Yosemite. The story of Kings Canyon National Park marks the triumph of Club advocacy over new obstacles: rival federal agencies and a split in the conservation movement over strategy and objectives.

The two main forks of the Kings River carve deep, dramatic canyons much like Yosemite as they flow west from the High Sierra just north of Sequoia National Park, which was established in 1890 and expanded in 1926. The Kings River country had been proposed as a national park since the days of Muir, but in the twenties and early thirties it got tangled up in an intramural dispute among the government's Forest Service and Park Service, the Sierra Club, and two other conservation organizations, the National Parks Association, an organization created to supplement the work of the National Park Service from outside government, and The Wilderness Society, founded to encourage the preservation of undeveloped wilderness areas.

Kings Canyon was just one instance among many where the two federal agencies saw themselves in competition. The Park Service, a part of the Interior Department, manages its lands for preservation and recreation: no commodity development is allowed. The Forest Service, part of the Agriculture Department, manages its lands to provide wood, recreation, wildlife habitat, and watershed protection. It does allow mining and grazing in addition to logging.

President Franklin Roosevelt, with Interior Secretary Harold Ickes leading the charge, wanted to establish a national park at Kings Canyon. The Forest Service, which would have to give up the land, resisted. The Sierra Club, which had for years publicly supported the general idea, was persuaded by the Forest Service that its new wilderness regulations were protection enough, and it lost enthusiasm for the park, especially since the park proposal omitted two major low-elevation valleys—Tehipite Valley and Cedar Grove—which were possible future reservoir sites and therefore a political problem in the task of garnering public support for the park. The two other conser-

David R. Brower. Richard Manning Leonard on an ascent of Arrowhead Spire in Yosemite Valley, 1937. Sierra Club Archives. A lawyer and rock climber, Dick Leonard may have served in high positions in more conservation organizations than any other Club member. He was a director of the Sierra Club for thirty-five years and spent two as president. Founder and first president of the Sierra Club Foundation, he was also a founder of the Conservation Law Society, of Trustees for Conservation, of American Conservation Films, and of the California chapter of the Izaak Walton League of America. He was vice chairman of the Committee on Legislation for the International Union for the Conservation of Nature and a long-time councillor of The Wilderness Society, similarly serving the Save-the-Redwood League for many years as director, president, and chairman.

Ansel Adams. William E. Colby, 1935 High Trip to Big Meadow and the Cartridge Creek region. © 1991 Trustees of the Ansel Adams Publishing Rights Trust. This portrait shows William Colby at age sixty on one of the thirty High Trips he led into the Sierra high country, Sierra Club excursions that he initiated in 1901.

vation organizations opposed the plan outright because of the omission of the two valleys and because of entreaties from the Forest Service to the effect that that agency would do a better job of preservation than the Park Service.

This latter argument was based on the fact that much Sierra Club-Park Service activity to that point had involved increased access to parks and potential parks. The Forest Service, sensing an imminent change of mood among conservationists to a desire for more pure, roadless wilderness, claimed it would leave the area wild. Purist conservationists were skeptical, having clashed frequently with the Forest Service on matters of logging and road building. They argued that the national park proposal should result in the establishment of Kings Canyon as a wilderness national park, under Park Service supervision, and would thus make it safer than it would be under the unpredictable management of the Forest Service. The omission of the lowland valleys was regrettable, but the time was right to protect the high country from a whole series of destructive hydroelectric dams. Tehipite and Cedar Grove could be added to the park later. Other conservationists were content to leave the area under Forest Service management.

Ickes, who is much admired by conservationists and considered by many to be, with Stewart Udall, our finest Interior Secretary, decided to light a fire under the Club. He traveled to San Francisco in October of 1938 and poured on the charm. He left with a bargain: the Club would support the park without the two valleys, and he would promise that the park would be devoted to wilderness, with no roads or hotels like those in Yosemite.

The battle to establish Kings Canyon National Park took place in the 1930s, and it produced the kind of multimedia collaboration the Club would pioneer and use so well in the future. In aid of the campaign, tasks were divided. Ansel Adams created a portfolio of photographs of the Kings Canyon

high country that the Sierra Club published as *Sierra Nevada: The John Muir Trail*. It was his first book. Will Colby wrote a pamphlet in the tradition of the many battle tracts he and Muir had brought out during the Hetch Hetchy struggle. Brower hoisted a twenty-pound Bell and Howell camera and produced the Sierra Club's first movie, *Sky-Land Trails of the Kings*, an hour-long, silent, color film shot principally during the High Trips of 1939 and 1940. These propaganda efforts, along with more traditional grassroots activities—lobbying and testifying and letter-writing—accomplished the goal: the Kings Canyon National Park legislation was passed by Congress and signed by President Roosevelt in 1940. Tehipite Valley and Cedar Grove were added to the park several years later, and to this day Kings Canyon remains the least developed national park outside Alaska.

❧

MOUNTAINEERS IN WARTIME

World War II found a reported one thousand Sierra Club members (of a total membership of around four thousand) in uniform, some of them using their mountaineering skills to train soldiers for the Italian campaign. These men would eventually push the German army back northward along the spine of Italy, across the Po Valley, and into surrender in the Italian Alps.

A Club director and later president, Bestor Robinson, served in Washington, D.C., in the office of the quartermaster general, helping to design military mountain equipment. Robinson was a self-described equipment fanatic who had been instrumental in introducing pitons, carabiners, expansion bolts, and other gadgets to Sierra Club climbers; he was right at home in the quartermaster's department of the Army. He got another director and future president, Dick Leonard, to join him.

Leonard, for his part, arranged that when Brower enlisted, he would be assigned to mountain-troop school in Colorado and then to officer-candidate school in Georgia. (A college dropout, Brower was not automatic officer material like Robinson and Leonard.) Many other Sierra Club mountaineers wound up in the celebrated Tenth Mountain Division as well, including Raffi Bedayn, Richard Emerson, Milton Hildebrand, Sandy Tepfer, and some who did not return: Art Argiewicz, Rus Lindsey, and Jack Benson among them.

David R. Brower. To prepare for World War II action in the European mountains, U.S. soldiers trained at the Seneca Assault Climbing School in West Virginia. Here, above and below, belay and rappel practice for soldiers who were Sierra Club members. 1944. Collection of David Brower

MIDDLE
David R. Brower. Sierra Club members Richard Emerson and Leo Healy at the base of a rock climb, Seneca Assault Climbing School, West Virginia. 1944. Collection of David Brower

The Club contingent wrote manuals and trained recruits in the techniques of rock climbing and camping in difficult terrain. Once the German army had been pushed out of North Africa, the mountain troops were sent to Italy in 1944 to carry the fighting into the hills. By May 1945, they, along with several other divisions, had pushed the Germans into Austria, and the war in Italy was ended. Brower, Bedayan, Hildebrand, and others took time off to climb in the Alps, at last just for fun.

Carr Clifton. Banner Peak, Thousand Island Lake, Ansel Adams Wilderness, California. 1989. In recognition of his tireless crusading on behalf of the environment, Ansel Adams's name is on the land in California, like Muir's and Will Colby's. Mount Ansel Adams, on the headwaters of the Lyell Fork of the Merced River in the Yosemite high country, was dedicated in fall 1984. The Ansel Adams Wilderness, in the Sierra and Inyo National Forests, was named in 1984 as well.

Ansel Adams. Bulldozers rupture the polished granite slopes above Tenaya Lake for the "new and improved" Tioga Road, a project opposed by Club leaders. 1959. © 1991 Trustees of the Ansel Adams Publishing Rights Trust

POLICY CHANGES IN PEACETIME

At the end of the war, as the nation slowly returned to a more normal way of life, the Sierra Club also turned again to its traditional activities. As noted, there were by then on the order of four thousand members, a board of directors, and committees to oversee outings, publishing, and conservation, all run by volunteers. A true professional staff was still some years in the future.

As it swung back into action, the board found itself resuming debate on difficult questions over outing policy: how many people is too many people in the mountains at one time? How can the impact of large outings be reduced? When, if ever, should elaborate ski resorts be allowed to invade wilderness areas? To address the former questions, the number of packstock on the High Trips had been cut in half by the late thirties, as gear was improved and lightened and planners realized that if camps were established closer together, pack teams could shuttle baggage twice a day rather than once. Burro trips had been instituted in 1937. These were cheaper, having no staff, and enjoyed the advantage of the fact that burros are far less damaging to meadows and woods than the mules that were used on the High Trips. Knapsack trips were begun as well, using four-footed helpers only to place food in caches in advance. The Base Camp trip originated in 1940, a creation of Club leaders from Southern California. For these trips, packers would tote campers' belongings to a campsite perhaps ten miles from a road head and leave the members there for two to four weeks, returning only to bring in supplies. These trips were particularly popular with families with children, who could be as active or inactive as they wanted once camp was made.

The Club had introduced thousands of people to the mountain wilderness; should it start thinking about limiting numbers? The original purpose of the Club had been "To explore, enjoy, and render accessible . . ." the mountains of the Pacific Coast, and the "render accessible" part had begun to worry people. In the twenties the Sierra Club had advocated the building of many roads across the Sierra to open up more wilderness to the public unwilling or unable to make the journey on foot—either their own or a horse's or mule's. The organization also advocated the building of trails, beginning with the John Muir Trail, to facilitate entry for hikers to remote areas. But now there were painful disagreements over road policy.

One such schism came with the establishment of Kings Canyon as a national park in 1940. A group in the Club wanted to build a road up the South Fork canyon to Copper Creek into the park. Leonard and Brower, among others, opposed the road as an unnecessary and odious intrusion into untouched country and argued that trails were the most the Club should support by way of access routes into any wilderness. But Will Colby was adamant. With other directors, he had promised a road to Copper Creek to

Philip Hyde. The Old Tioga Road along Lake Tenaya. 1949. Sierra Club Archives. This narrow road respected the topography of the lake area, unlike the new one, blasted across the granite slopes by the Park Service in 1959.

David R. Brower. A Sierra Club ski expedition follows the old Tioga Road through Lee Vining Canyon on the east side of the Sierra Nevada, winter of 1936–37. Collection of David Brower

win support of the park among citizens in Fresno, and he prevailed, even though a report by Frederick Law Olmsted, Jr., had recommended against it. The road was built, to accommodate the fast-growing number of automobile recreationists.

A WRONG TURN ON THE TIOGA ROAD

The quarrel over a road into Kings Canyon highlights the Club's fundamental internal disagreement over strategy and purpose in the 1940s. Opposition flared most awkwardly when the Park Service decided to "improve" the road from Crane Flat to Tioga Pass in Yosemite National Park. (When bureaucrats use that word, it means, in most cases, to "straighten, pave, flatten, and generally to shorten the time it takes to traverse" a stretch of road, not necessarily an improvement to roads that pass through particularly scenic country.)

The old Yosemite road was there before the park was enlarged in 1890, having been built to provide access to a mine that went bust before the road was ever put into service. It snaked and meandered at a leisurely pace up the swales and around the ridges, avoiding the most beautiful lakes and respecting the magnificent polished granite slopes that are the particular glory of the Yosemite high country.

The Park Service wanted to change all that, to make Tuolumne Meadows, Lake Tenaya, and Tioga Pass accessible to people who were probably in too much of a hurry to look at them. The last leg to remain unimproved was the stretch through the Tenaya basin, the site of one of the most beautiful lakes in a range that has an embarrassment of beautiful ones. The Park Service proposed blasting a new roadbed across the glacier-polished granite on the south and west sides of the lake, an act that would later be described as scenic vandalism.

The Club felt ambivalent, at least collectively. Its board had endorsed upgrading, but not realigning, the road as far back as 1934. Individually, most directors felt strongly, one way or another. As would happen again, over and over, there were matters of principle that seemed to be in conflict. One was preservationist. Its adherents felt that the Sierra Club was duty-bound to protect as much wilderness as possible in all circumstances. The other felt that "render accessible" meant cooperating in schemes to develop wilderness to provide convenient entry to large numbers of people. Board members also believed that they had reached an agreement to cooperate with the Park Service in the improvement of the Tioga road and that they must stick by this agreement. This allegiance to old agreements, and their subsequent reinterpretation, would flare again and again as the Club grew, society at large grew, pressure on wild places grew, and issues like access to wilderness became more and more complex.

The improvement of the Tioga road presented such a dilemma. Should the Club stand firm and oppose this further opening up of the Yosemite high country, or should it go along, in order to render the land accessible and stick by its earlier position? Harold Bradley, the son of a Sierra Club founder, who would serve a decade on the board, including two years as president, and Dave Brower argued against the last realignment in the *Sierra Club Bulletin* in 1949. The board temporized, deciding that what it really needed was a general, overall policy statement for national park roads. In the end the Club did oppose the blasting of the road through Tenaya's polished apron, but it was too late. Plans were fixed and construction had continued. Vacillation had permitted the rupturing of magnificent polished faces, a destruction that was in fact unnecessary, even conceding the goal of remaking the road to allow faster travel. The lesson of the Tioga road was not to be forgotten soon among Sierra Club leaders.

❧

COLLISION COURSE
OVER SKIING

At about the same time the Club was embroiled in another issue of public policy and wilderness recreation that would be solved in a way that would later turn and bite the organization. The subject this time was skiing and the rendering accessible of a remote mountain valley.

In the mountains east of Los Angeles is the San Gorgonio Wild Area, a precious oasis of undisturbed mountain country close to that densely popu-

130

lated region. In the mid-forties the Forest Service proposed to permit construction of a ski resort to serve the growing demand for skiing opportunities by people who lived in the desert climate of Southern California and were weary of having to drive a further five hours to reach the nearest developed ski area, at Mammoth Mountain on the east side of the Sierra.

Sierra Club leaders were divided on the San Gorgonio ski proposal, and the Winter Sports Committee and the Club president approved it. But Brower in one vigorous night of lobbying persuaded a majority of the directors to oppose it.

In an effort to cooperate with the Forest Service and the skiing public, and since skiing of all kinds was growing in popularity among Club members themselves, the Club mounted a survey of its own to find other areas that might be appropriately developed as ski resorts, thinking that it might be able to keep resorts away from the places where they would do the most damage.

In general, such surveys are part of a strategy with a great deal of surface appeal. When it works well, a solution is found that most closely pleases all parties. It also gives the organization—the Sierra Club in this case—the chance to be helpful and constructive rather than simply obstructionist, as its opponents like to claim. But the strategy generally involves the likelihood of compromise, which a pressure group like the Sierra Club is not always willing to agree to. And it carries the possibility of alienating some fraction of the group's members, who may disagree with the "constructive" alternative held out as a substitute for the area sought by the developer. It is a tricky path at best.

In any event, in an attempt to be helpful and constructive—and to save San Gorgonio—two Sierra Club volunteers made an aerial reconnaissance of the southern Sierra in search of sites for ski-resort development. Their consensus, reported in an article in the *Bulletin*, was that the most promising possibility was at Mineral King, a small valley about equidistant from San Francisco and Los Angeles. It had just the right sort of slopes and bowls and plenty of snow. The main drawback was that access to the valley was by an unpaved old wagon road that was narrow and serpentine and would have to be enormously improved before it could be used in winter. The road also passed through Sequoia National Park on its way to Mineral King, which had been left in Sequoia National Forest when the park was expanded in 1926 because of old derelict mines.

In 1949 the Board boiled down its committee's report to a resolution to the effect that the Club would not oppose the use of Mineral King as a ski resort, a decision it would come to reexamine heatedly—and eventually to reverse—in years to come.

In 1951 the Club's Board decided it had better bring the statement of the official purposes of the Club in line with modern realities. Where the original purposes had been, "To explore, enjoy, and render accessible the mountain regions of the Pacific Coast . . . ," the amended version became, "To explore, enjoy, and protect the Sierra Nevada and other scenic resources of the United

Edward T. Parsons. Center Basin, Kings Canyon National Park, during the 1910 High Trip. Sierra Club Archives

In support of the creation of Kings Canyon National Park, Will Colby wrote a powerful pamphlet, pointing out that, "This Club has always stood for the ideal that a true National Park is a primeval wilderness area of supreme scenic beauty, a conspicuous example of Nature's handiwork upon a scale large enough to be of national importance, and eminently worthy of complete preservation for the inspiration of present and future generations, and for the recreation of the American people." The Park was created in 1940.

States." The rendering accessible could be left to others. Indeed, the Club would spend far more of its time in the future trying to block various attempts to build new accessways into wilderness than it would supporting them.

CONFERRING
FOR WILDERNESS

It is a peculiarly American phenomenon that the preservation of nature's status quo — wilderness — would become a political movement, but it did, because wilderness was defenseless and needed the power of law for its protection. The English Romantics sang the praises of nature; Americans translated lyric poetry into hard-nosed law. The wilderness movement that the Sierra Club helped pioneer and direct in the latter nineteenth century grew swiftly in the early twentieth.

The father of the American wilderness movement is generally thought to be Aldo Leopold, who served two decades in the U.S. Forest Service beginning in 1909, later occupying the first chair in wildlife management in the country, at the University of Wisconsin. Leopold never joined the Sierra Club

Galen Rowell. Moonrise from the Summit of Mount Whitney, California. 1988. Steve Roper and Allen Steck's *Fifty Classic Climbs* describes the first successful ascent of Mount Whitney from the east, by a Sierra Club party in 1931: "It was mid-morning on August 16. . . . The two younger climbers [Jules Eichorn and Glen Dawson] suggested a frontal attack, but, as [Robert] Underhill put it, 'before such a tour de force was undertaken [Norman] Clyde and I urged that a traverse . . . be investigated. Clyde later wrote that this traverse 'proved to be one requiring considerable steadiness, as the ledges were narrow and there was a thousand feet of fresh air below.' The now famous Fresh-Air Traverse generally is regarded as the crux of the route. . . . At the 14,200-foot level . . . pausing when out of breath to gaze at the astonishingly clear vista . . . 'even the Californians did not succeed in remaining impeccably blasé about the view.' "

and in fact had little experience in the West. Nevertheless, his ideas on wilderness had a profound influence on the development of the Club's philosophy, and Club leaders worked closely with leaders of The Wilderness Society, a membership organization that Leopold cofounded in 1934. For them, wilderness was the ideal to preserve. Parks might have scenery, but parks could also have roads, cabins, and other human contrivances. Wilderness had no permanent human structures. It represented the forces that had shaped life on earth for billions of years before the first humans. It was, in the words of some now-anonymous wag, "where the hand of man had not set foot."

Leopold's seminal work is *A Sand County Almanac*, published posthumously in 1948. His second book, *Round River*, another collection of essays published in 1953, contains the following passage, which has been quoted sympathetically in many Club publications and could still serve as a motto for people working to preserve the natural world.

> The last word in ignorance is the man who says of an animal or plant: "What good is it?" If the land mechanism as a whole is good, then every part is good, whether we understand it or not. If the biota, in the course of aeons, has built something we like but do not understand, then who but a fool would discard seemingly useless parts? To keep every cog and wheel is the first precaution of intelligent tinkering.[20]

Leopold's counterpart in founding the Society was Robert Marshall, another professional forester. They designed the Society to be a public support group for the Forest Service, much as the National Parks Association was created to provide support for the National Park Service. Marshall remained an employee of the service, serving as Chief of Recreation and Lands at the time of his death in 1939. Both men spoke for others in wondering openly how wilderness might best be protected, how much might be withdrawn from possible development for minerals, lumber, water, or power; what mechanisms might be put into place to protect wilderness; and what sort of agency should manage it—insofar as wilderness would need any management at all.

Leopold and Marshall hoped the Forest Service would be a leader in protecting wilderness, and the two did persuade the agency to declare many areas wilderness and off-limits to most development. When asked to support permanent legal protection for the areas, however, the agency balked. Its ties to the timber, mining, and livestock industries were too strong. Statutory protection would have to be forced upon the Forest Service and other federal land-management agencies if such protection was to become a reality.

By the late forties, more than a decade after The Wilderness Society came into being, wilderness supporters decided that a series of conferences might help nudge along the slow-moving process of fashioning legal preservation for wilderness.

The idea for the wilderness conference is generally credited to Norman B. ("Ike") Livermore, Jr., a man who entered the Club on horseback rather than through mountaineering. Livermore, who would later serve as California's Secretary of Resources under Governor Ronald Reagan, had been a packer and had escorted many Sierra Club High Trips before—and after—joining the Club's Board of Directors in 1941. Livermore thought the Club could profitably play host to a conference that would bring together citizens and leaders from the Park Service, the Forest Service, appropriate state agencies, and others to discuss policies for protecting wild country.

The first of the biennial conferences was held in 1949; at the second, in 1951, Howard Zahniser, The Wilderness Society's distinguished leader, made the first public appeal for a federal law to grant permanent protection to wilderness areas. The idea was to go through many revisions until it was enacted more than a decade later, and the conferences would play a major role in bringing together the people who made it happen.

The conferences would continue until 1975. The list of participants is a virtual roster of the conservation establishment of that era, with a liberal sprinkling of government officials, politicians, and resource scientists. Conferences were organized around themes, including "The Meaning of Wilderness to Science" and "Wilderness, the Edge of Knowledge." Proceedings were published in book form and sold to members and libraries. Speakers, panelists, and the audience wrestled with questions both practical and philosophical. As David Brower summed up in his foreword to the proceedings of the sixth conference,

> [During the first six conferences] there was growing conviction that wilderness could enhance the American standard of living—if the American standard of *having* did not extinguish wilderness first. It was postulated that if America were to ignore, for utilitarian purposes, that small part of its land area which is still wilderness, if America were to consider it there just to be enjoyed for what it is and not for what

Robert McCabe. Aldo Leopold. 1950s. University of Wisconsin–Madison Archives, Madison, Wisconsin. Author of *A Sand County Almanac,* Aldo Leopold was a leading exponent of the wilderness idea. He profoundly influenced the Club, though his contact was mainly through his sons A. Starker and Luna. A. Starker Leopold, one of the leading wildlife biologists of his time, taught at the University of California at Berkeley, served on the Club's board from 1954 to 1960, and in the early 1960s produced an influential report on wildlife management for the Department of the Interior. Luna Leopold was a Club board member in 1968–71 when he was chief scientist for the U.S. Geological Survey. A hydrologist, he invented a widely used formula for predicting how far sand and silt will back up behind a reservoir on a muddy river.

Carr Clifton. Center Peak and Mount Stanford, Kings Canyon National Park, California. 1989

it could be remodeled into, then the nation would still survive hand-somely — perhaps even more so. Just pretend it isn't there, the theory runs, and carry on business as usual *around* it; you won't regret it. There isn't too much heresy in the concept. Successful corporations call it a reserve. A successfully civilized nation ought to be able to set aside a reserve, not of money for a rainy day, but of wilderness for a rainy century — and enjoy it *as wilderness* until the rains come or even beyond that.[21]

Brower recounted proposals put forward and refined at preceding confer-ences, for the reform of the National Park Service, of the Forest Service and forestry, of the management of wildlife and water resources, and of the con-duct of the builders of roads and highways. The appeal was not only esthetic, but practical as well, as Brower makes explicit:

> We have lately been playing a game of strip poker with the American earth. A relatively few people have been winning the early hands — people interested in quick profits for the sake of conveniences — and all but guaranteeing that our children will lose as the game goes on, not just conveniences, but necessities as well.

Wilderness — the enjoyment of it, the preservation of it — would remain the principal preoccupation of the Sierra Club and The Wilderness Society for many years. The Wilderness Conferences were instrumental in focusing ef-forts that would one day see the establishment of the world's first national wilderness preservation system.

Jeff Gnass. Little Redfish Lake
Reflections, Mount Heyburn, Sawtooth
Range, Idaho. 1984

THE CLUB
COMES OF AGE

❦

ENTERING THE MODERN ERA
OF CONSERVATION
1950 ❦ 1970

B y 1950 the Sierra Club had passed a couple of significant milestones. The first—following its founding in 1892—was the initiation of the High Trip and the maturing of the organization as a dual-purpose force for outings and conservation. The second was the death of the founder and first president, John Muir. Then, at mid-century, another collection of factors coincided that would again profoundly affect the shape, personality, and mission of the institution, by then fifty-eight years old.

The Club by 1950 had a few less than seven thousand members, most of them on the West Coast, and nine chapters, all in California. It was little known outside its home territory, except to officials of the federal conservation agencies and to politicians who had to vote on matters within the Club's sphere of interest. Since the struggles for Hetch Hetchy and Yosemite, the Club had not been much in evidence nationally. That was all to change rapidly, as chapters began to be established in the East and elsewhere and the political focus of the Club's activities once again ranged beyond California.

As mentioned near the end of chapter two, the Club's directors had finally decided that the official purpose of the organization should no longer include efforts to "render accessible" wilderness and other undeveloped natural areas, so the organization was free to take a more absolute position with regard to all kinds of development proposals. There were plenty of such proposals being put forward, at an accelerating pace.

Following the end of World War II, with the return of thousands of soldiers from Europe and the Pacific and the final recovery of the economy from the Great Depression, the demand for natural resources soared. Timber for houses was harvested at a swiftly increasing rate, which threw conservationists into more and more conflict with the Forest Service and the timber industry. The Sierra Club had had uncongenial dealings with that agency before; they would intensify and occupy a growing amount of the Club's time and effort as the years wore on.

The GIs and their young families needed not only wood for new homes, but also places to build them, and many were drawn to the Southwest and to California. Once the houses were built—alongside shops, schools, factories, and other buildings—electricity was needed to run lights, refrigerators, televisions, and myriad other new appliances. This led to protracted conflict

as well, since an altogether environmentally benign method of generating electricity has yet to be invented. The method of choice in those days, at least where cooperative rivers were available, was the hydroelectric dam. One project in particular would serve to drag the Sierra Club onto the national stage again, where it would stay permanently. It was the Colorado River Storage Project.

In 1922, under the terms of the Colorado River Compact, the Colorado River basin had been arbitrarily divided into upper and lower halves, the dividing line running between the Grand Canyon and Glen Canyon at the Arizona-Utah border. The Upper Basin project, a creation of the federal Bureau of Reclamation, was the portion that first snared the Club's attention. The main features of this proposal were seven power and water-storage dams, including the Curicanti on the Gunnison River, the Navajo on the San Juan, the Cross Mountain on the Yampa (still not built today), the Flaming Gorge on the Green, the Glen Canyon on the Colorado, and two—Echo Park and Split Mountain—within Dinosaur National Monument on the Green River. The Club was most disturbed by the Split Mountain and Echo Park dams because of their location inside a national monument: the project was a replay of Hetch Hetchy and the organization was viscerally opposed to allowing construction.

To mount the campaign that would be necessary to tackle a project of this magnitude—particularly as it was situated in Utah, a long way from headquarters and from the Club's core of support—the directors decided to hire David Brower as the Club's first executive director. There had been employees before—caretakers, outings guides, membership clerks, even part-time conservation activists including Brower himself. But when Brower began as the Club's executive director at the close of 1952, his employment marked the beginning of the Sierra Club as a professionally staffed organization.

Brower was well acquainted with the Club. He had been a member nearly twenty years, had led numerous High Trips, knapsack trips, and other excursions, had been editor of the *Bulletin*, and had served on the board of directors since 1941. Following his discharge from active military service, he had returned to his job as an editor with the University of California Press, but he continued to devote countless hours to Sierra Club projects.

❧

THE BATTLE FOR DINOSAUR

The federal government has two dam-building agencies: the Army Corps of Engineers and the Bureau of Reclamation, the child of Major John Wesley Powell.[22] The Corps, a branch of the military, and the Bureau, part of the Interior Department, often compete for projects to build, just as the Forest Service and the Park Service compete for land to manage. These agencies, and private developers, had already dammed many of the obvious sites by 1950. There were dams on the streams flowing out of the Sierra Nevada and the southern Cascades, irrigating the Great Valley of California at the cost of

destroying one of the greatest systems of seasonal wetlands anywhere in the world. Dams on the rivers of California's North Coast and in the Pacific Northwest, including most notably the mighty Columbia, were ruining the salmon fisheries that were once so plentiful there, just as dams in the East had ruined fisheries there a century before. At the end of the war, the Bureau focused its gaze on the arid regions of the upper Colorado plateau, to see what would grow in the desert, given water from the river at just the right time.

This is marginal land for irrigated agriculture, at best. Elevations are high, the weather harsh, the growing season short. Irrigation projects there would be hard to justify economically by themselves, so the Bureau devised what it called "cash register" dams, which would earn money by selling electricity and underwrite the irrigation schemes with any surplus profit.

Two of these cash register dams were pencilled onto maps on the Green River inside Dinosaur National Monument. The upper dam, at a spot known as Echo Park for the grand reverberations the sandstone cliffs could generate, would be used for peaking power—demand that comes in surges as, for example, when everybody in Salt Lake City turns on their appliances at the same time. To meet this demand, a great deal of water is released in a short period. This may produce the cooling sought by residents of Salt Lake City, but when great tsunamis of water charge down the riverbed downstream of a peaking-power dam, they make a mess, washing away beaches and siltbars and ripping up trees and shrubs. They destroy wildlife habitat as well. To lessen this problem, the Bureau suggested a second, "reregulating," dam twenty-five miles downstream from Echo Park, at Split Mountain, a spectacular spot where the river plunges through a mountain that the ancient river clove in twain as it rose slowly upward. The Split Mountain dam would capture the surges from Echo Park, limiting downstream damage, and give the Bureau a second opportunity to sell power, though this would be of the base-load variety, that is, slow and steady rather than the on-again, off-again peaking sort.

In any event, all these niceties were irrelevant to the big question: whether power and water, as needed as they might or might not be, should take precedence over preserving the integrity of the National Park System in general and the beauty of Dinosaur National Monument in particular.

The Sierra Club launched its biggest campaign since Hetch Hetchy—in fact, an even bigger one since the organization had by then many more members and more resources.

Using a technique from its past, the Club undertook to set people working by making them familiar with the resource at stake. It hired the legendary river-runner Bus Hatch to float people though the canyons of Dinosaur, a first experience for most of them in those magnificent, remote expanses of slickrock and willow, cottonwood and maidenhair fern. Two hundred individuals floated Dinosaur that summer of 1953. Ordinary citizens made the trip. So did politicians and journalists. All three groups represented a long-term investment by the Club: those attracted to the Club's way of thinking by the trip through Dinosaur would stay interested in conservation through the rest of their lives. The journalists would be much better attuned to the Club's arguments on these matters and more likely to lend an unbiased ear — even a sympathetic one — to the organization's entreaties.

This was a particularly important part of the Club's overall strategy. The government, on the one hand, especially the Bureau of Reclamation, cultivated the image of a leading expert on resource-management issues. If a Bureau of Reclamation engineer said something was true, it often seemed beyond cavil — never mind what a conservationist might claim. Forest Service foresters enjoyed the same deference. Nature lovers, as the defenders of Hetch Hetchy were sneeringly called, were accused of bleeding their hearts out over cuddly creatures and postcard views, but about the really important things — supplying electricity to consumers and water to farmers — the government's experts held themselves out as the highest authority. Reporters, on the other hand, might plant the idea that the government was not perfect. Indeed, one government agency was to be shown up badly before the Dinosaur battle finally ended.

A pivotal point came in January 1954, when Brower made an appearance before the House Committee on Interior and Insular Affairs, which was considering legislation to authorize the Upper Colorado River Storage Project, including the Echo Park, Split Mountain, Flaming Gorge, and Glen Canyon dams. Brower gave a luminous description of his first visits to the canyon the previous summer — with camera and a party of two hundred — and then proceeded to accuse the Bureau of Reclamation of making mistakes in simple algebra. The key dispute was about whether more water would be lost to evaporation with dams at Glen, Echo Park, and Split Mountain or with a single, higher dam at Glen Canyon. The Bureau insisted that the three-dam plan would best conserve water in that arid land. Brower pointed to what he insisted were errors in the Bureau's figures and stressed that the single-dam, "Big Glen" option would be better in that respect. The agency, he averred, had miscalculated the surface area of the combined Echo Park, Split Mountain, and "little Glen" reservoirs.

Congressmen on the committee — particularly Wayne Aspinall of Colorado, a vigorous champion of the Bureau and a steadfast reclamationeer — were aghast that Brower would challenge the figures. They had been calculated by the professional engineers of the Bureau of Reclamation and presented by the Under Secretary of the Interior, Ralph Tudor, who testified for the project and was one of the principal engineers on the San Francisco Bay Bridge, completed in 1937. "If Mr. Tudor is such a poor engineer as you seem to claim he is, I am surprised he ever got that . . . bridge down in your town to meet at the center," commented committee member William Dawson of Utah. Brower made no claim to being an engineer and confessed that he had learned his algebra in the ninth grade. But he was finally proved right and the Bureau wrong. The agency had indeed miscalculated the surface area of the various reservoirs and therefore their evaporation rates. This was too much for the *Salt Lake Tribune*, until then a supporter of the dams. It awarded the Bureau's regional director a rubber slide rule "for stretching the truth."

Arthur Schatz. David Brower takes a farewell trip through Glen Canyon in 1966, as the waters of Lake Powell were rising, appearing in a story that year in a national magazine. Foreground, left to right: John Brower, Paul Davidson, Barbara Brower. David Brower's Sierra Club career began with mountaineering in the 1930s, then included magazine editing and a decade on the board of directors in the forties. In 1952 he became the Club's first executive director and led successful opposition to dams in Dinosaur National Monument and the Grand Canyon. He conceived and promoted the Exhibit Format series of illustrated books. His stormy seventeen-year career on the Club's staff ended in 1969, but he returned to serve two three-year terms on the board in the 1980s, was elected an honorary vice president, and received the Club's highest award, named for Muir.

Ansel Adams. Rock and Grass, Moraine
Lake, Sequoia National Park, California.
1932. © 1991 Trustees of the Ansel
Adams Publishing Rights Trust

Having beaten back and even embarrassed the Bureau of Reclamation at the hearings, the Sierra Club turned its attention toward building public support for its position on Dinosaur. The national monument was little known, and most people undoubtedly thought of it as the site of dinosaur skeletons. It is that, of course, but it is also the site of wide expanses of beautiful sandstone wilderness. To save it from the dams, the public would have to be educated and aroused about the values at stake at Dinosaur National Monument.

Accordingly, the techniques used in behalf of Kings Canyon were resurrected and improved. Club volunteers skilled in cinematography filmed the float trips through Dinosaur that summer, and turned the footage into a film called *Wilderness River Trail*. They later produced a second film as well, *Two Yosemites*, which showed the repellent mess of the reservoir in Hetch Hetchy and pleaded that the same fate not befall Dinosaur. At the same time, Wallace Stegner, author of a history of the Powell exploration of the Colorado in 1869, agreed to edit a book on Dinosaur and the dam controversy, to be published by Alfred A. Knopf. *This Is Dinosaur* married texts by experts in several pertinent fields with photographs in color and black-and-white of the places at risk in the Dinosaur campaign. Brower recruited the authors — an anthropologist, a geologist, a river-runner, and others. Alfred Knopf wrote the final chapter himself. Five thousand copies were printed and one quickly found its way to the desk of each member of Congress. The Club had used the printed word and photography in the service of conservation often before, in the *Bulletin*, in pamphlets during the Hetch Hetchy campaign, and in Ansel Adams's book published for the Kings Canyon National Park campaign. *This Is Dinosaur* was the most ambitious publication to date. There was more, far more, to come.

Using their influence and contacts in the world of journalism, the Club leaders and their allies helped inspire popular magazines and newspapers to report on the Dinosaur controversy. Articles appeared in *Life*, *National Geographic*, and other periodicals. The *Los Angeles Times* carried numerous pieces on the matter, many of them by Martin Litton, who also assisted in filming the Club's movies. Litton would serve on the Club's board in future years, and be a key player in many conservation battles. John Oakes, editorial page editor of *The New York Times*, weighed in with editorials supporting the conservationists' position. Oakes would also serve on the Club's board and on the governing body of the Natural Resources Defense Council into the 1990s, becoming one of the most compelling and consistent voices for conservation in the country.

By late 1955 the conservationists seemed to be gaining the upper hand. The techniques outlined above had roused Club members and other members of the public, who peppered their senators and congressmen with letters and telegrams. Sierra Club lobbyists then reported an interesting phenomenon. When previously they had asked for appointments with legislators to discuss the Dinosaur dams, they were often rebuffed or ignored by solons who had never heard of Dinosaur and had more important matters on their minds. Once the legislator received a handful of letters from constituents, however, he or she was far more receptive to what the Sierra Club representative had to say. The power of the grassroots was palpable. It was slowly turning the tide.

Though the Senate had approved a bill authorizing the Upper Basin Project on the Colorado with the Echo Park project included, the House had not, and support for the dams was fading fast. The conservationists turned up the heat. Brower and Litton collaborated on a special issue of the *Sierra Club Bulletin* devoted wholly to Dinosaur. They explained the Club's position and the rationale for it. They urged readers to make their views known to members of Congress and to the editors of their local newspapers, which they did, in large numbers.

In June 1954, as the fight was under way on several fronts, the U.S. Supreme Court (*U.S. v. Harriss*, Chief Justice Warren writing for the majority, Justices Douglas, Black, and Jackson in dissent) ruled that it was illegal for organizations that solicited tax-deductible donations from their members and others to use that money to influence legislation pending before Congress. Or, if such lobbying was not wholly illegal, the Court suggested that Congress and the Internal Revenue Service could limit its extent. It was the opening shot in a skirmish over the use of charitable contributions to support lobbying efforts, a legal point that would be revived a decade later and used against the Club in another controversy.

As a direct result of the *Harriss* decision, a new non-tax-deductible organization was formed by Dick Leonard and other Club leaders called Trustees for Conservation to solicit money that could legally be used for lobbying. In the East, the leaders of major conservationist organizations—all tax-deductible and therefore shackled by *Harriss*—formed the Citizens Committee on Natural Resources. A third new organization, the Council of Conservationists, also formed in order to lobby, was governed by the chief executive officers of the Club, The Wilderness Society, the Izaak Walton League, and the Wildlife Management Institute. The Council soon made history, pioneering a technique that would be used to tremendous advantage by the Sierra Club and other organizations in the following years: the full-page newspaper ad.

On Halloween in 1955 the supporters and sponsors of the Colorado River Storage Project—the Upper Basin Strategy Committee—were scheduled to meet in Denver to plan strategy. When they awakened that morning, they found a full-page advertisement, an open letter addressed to them in the *Denver Post*. In it, the Council of Conservationists enumerated their arguments against the Echo Park project and the flaws in the Bureau of Reclamation's rationale for it. They said they were prepared to exert efforts to scuttle the entire Upper Basin Project if Echo Park was not removed from it. And they observed that the public was passionately interested in this matter and that the reelection chances of certain congressmen would not be enhanced by their support of such an unpopular cause.

The ad forced the committee members to confront reality—the Dinosaur

proposal was doomed for lack of support. Two days later the Upper Basin Strategy Committee agreed to drop the Echo Park/Split Mountain project from the bill, and by the end of November Interior Secretary Douglas McKay had dropped the dams from the Upper Basin Project altogether. (At the time conservationists referred to the Secretary as "Giveaway McKay" for his evident intention to give away Dinosaur, and perhaps other elements of the park system, to the Bureau of Reclamation.) McKay resigned the next day. The conservationists agreed not to oppose the other elements of the project.

҂

THE PLACE NO ONE KNEW

In the months leading up to the victory for Dinosaur, some conservationist leaders worried that they might be giving up Glen Canyon too easily in order to save the national monument. Glen, on the main stem of the Colorado in southern Utah, had been visited by almost nobody. John Wesley Powell, on his exploration trip in 1869, had found it a superlatively magnificent place, with a far gentler Colorado River than existed in Grand Canyon and the most sublime side canyons to be seen anywhere in creation. He reported,

> On the walls, and back many miles into the country, numbers of monument-shaped buttes are observed. So we have a curious *ensemble* of wonderful features — carved walls, royal arches, glens, alcove gulches, mounds, and monuments. From which of these features shall we select a name? We decide to call it Glen Canyon....
>
> Past these towering monuments, past these mounded billows of orange sandstone, past these oak-set glens, past these fern-decked al- coves, past these mural curves, we glide hour after hour, stopping now and then, as our attention is arrested by some new wonder....[23]

How, the conservationists asked themselves, can we agree to a project that will inundate a place we have never visited? And the few who *had* seen Glen Canyon suggested that it ought to be a national park itself.

The other side argued that saving Dinosaur National Monument was all they could hope for, and since Glen Canyon was not a national park or monument, that a powerful argument for its preservation was missing from the equation. In the end, the organizations elected to let Glen be sacrificed in order to save Dinosaur, a decision most of them now deeply regret. Dave Brower wrote:

> Glen Canyon died in 1963 and I was partly responsible for its need- less death. So were you. Neither you nor I, nor anyone else, knew it well enough to insist that at all costs it should endure. When we began to find out it was too late. On January 21, 1963, the last day on which the execution of one of the planet's greatest scenic an- tiquities could yet have been stayed, the man who theoretically had the power to save this place [Secretary of the Interior Stewart Udall] did not pick up a telephone and give the necessary order. I was

within a few feet of his desk in Washington that day and witnessed how the forces long at work finally had their way. So a steel gate dropped, choking off the flow in the canyon's carotid artery, and from that moment the canyon's life force ebbed quickly. A huge reservoir, absolutely not needed in this century, almost certainly not needed in the next, and conceivably never to be needed at all, began to fill.[24]

Brower believes that the conservationists had reached a position of such strength by the mid-fifties that they could have killed the Upper Basin Project altogether if they had but tried. He quotes two senators who were astonished when the Sierra Club withdrew its opposition to the bill after Echo Park was removed. In any event, the Club did withdraw its opposition and the bill passed swiftly. A scant six months later the destruction of Glen Canyon began when President Eisenhower pushed a button in the White House, which triggered a charge of dynamite buried in the wall of the Canyon. The Glen Canyon Dam, and Lake Powell behind it, remains a powerful symbol to conservationists of environmental tragedy, high on the list of errors to be corrected as enlightenment grows in the future.

John V. Young. Cottonwood thicket in upper Lake Canyon, Glen Canyon, drowned in the early 1960s by the rising waters of Lake Powell. Sierra Club Archives

❧

FORESTS AND THE WILDERNESS IDEA

If the Bureau of Reclamation believed itself to be the supreme authority on rivers and streams, the Forest Service was of a similar mind when it came to trees. Conflicting philosophies about land use—Muir's esthetic approach versus Pinchot's utilitarianism—caused increasing friction between the Sierra Club and its kindred organizations on one side and the Forest Service and timber industry on the other. The quintessence of the disagreement arose over the idea of wilderness, that certain areas either exceptionally beautiful or representative of unique ecological communities should be preserved in a pristine condition, with almost no destructive activity allowed within them—no logging, no mining, no building of shelters, no construction of roads.

The conservationists saw wilderness as a reservoir of freedom, of the genetic heritage of all life, as habitat for wildlife, and as a spot for the recreation of body and spirit. The postwar Forest Service saw the wilderness as a potential source of lumber, minerals, and forage, and spoke of conservationists wanting to "lock up" the wilderness for the pleasure of a self-selected few.

In the between-the-wars period, the Forest Service had been a fairly conservation-minded agency, having withdrawn thousands of acres from logging and dubbed them "wilderness," or "primitive areas," or "research reserves," all with slightly different purposes and characteristics but all off-limits to logging. These areas did not have the same protection as national parks, which were created by law, but they were safe so long as the rulers of the agency wanted to keep them safe. The first formal wilderness—the Gila in Arizona—was established by the Forest Service under the influence of Aldo Leopold in 1924. The Wilderness Society's cofounder and Forest Service official Robert

Marshall influenced the establishment of others.

Following World War II, returning servicemen were hoping to build their first homes, which boosted demand for lumber. This, combined with the fact that forests on privately owned land had been ruthlessly stripped, led the managers of the national forests to declare that they would start harvesting more trees on federal lands and might reassess the lands that had been withdrawn as wilderness and primitive areas.

When the Forest Service announced in 1951 that it planned to declassify much of the forested land in the Three Sisters Primitive Area in Oregon, it added considerable urgency to the growing call for a Wilderness Act to give such lands permanent protection. Previous Forest Service administrators had set aside a primitive area in the Three Sisters, including not only the basalt and snow at the tops of the peaks, but also the heavily forested western ridges and valleys, 53,000 acres much prized by hikers and fishermen as well as loggers. The area had no statutory protection, just the "primitive area" designation, which the Secretary of Agriculture could withdraw in a minute.

Oregon conservationists, aided by the Club's Brower and Dr. Edgar Wayburn, fought the plan, raising public awareness but failing to dissuade the agriculture secretary, who declassified all 53,000 acres in 1957. The fight raged for two decades, until much of the area remaining unlogged, including French Pete Creek and two other valleys, was protected as wilderness.

One future Club leader who cut his teeth on the Three Sisters fight was Mike McCloskey. He had grown up in Eugene, Oregon, in the heart of timber country. He earned a degree in American government at Harvard, spent two years in the Army, then returned to Eugene to attend law school. As a law student in the late 1950s, he combined keen interests in politics and conservation, becoming friends with Oregon's senators, Richard Neuberger and Wayne Morse.

In 1959, McCloskey attended a meeting of the Federation of Western Outdoor Clubs, of which the Sierra Club was a leading member. McCloskey was the delegate from a Eugene outdoor club called the Obsidians. David Brower was also at the meeting, and was much impressed with the young law student from Oregon. McCloskey, for his part, was drawn to Brower's passion and vision; the two became friends. Brower asked McCloskey if he would come to work on the Club's payroll in the summer of 1960 to fight the Minam battle. McCloskey agreed.

Immediately following his graduation from law school in 1961, McCloskey came to work full-time as the conservation field representative for the Sierra Club, the Federation of Western Outdoor Clubs, the North Cascades Conservation Council, and several other organizations. He would go on to become the Club's first conservation director, second executive director, and first chairman.

In addition to fighting the specific battles — Three Sisters, Minam River, and others — Club leaders grew more convinced there must be a statutory way to protect wilderness. Forest Service wilderness areas could be opened to logging at the whim of the agency, and it was painfully clear that the

THE PLACE NO ONE KNEW
Glen Canyon on the Colorado
by ELIOT PORTER

Eliot Porter. Redbud in Bloom, Hidden Passage, Glen Canyon, Utah, April 1963. Courtesy of the Eliot Porter Archives, Amon Carter Museum, Fort Worth, Texas. This tender close-up, published in Porter's The Place No One Knew: Glen Canyon on the Colorado, epitomizes one of the photographer's signature approaches to nature. In a period when color photography was often grandiloquent and garish, he chose to frame an intimate view of nature with a few hues.

Eliot Porter's The Place No One Knew, 1963, was the fifth in the Exhibit Format series of Sierra Club books.

THIS IS THE
AMERICAN EARTH

ANSEL ADAMS & NANCY NEWHALL

The Eloquent Light

Sierra Club Bulletin   April 1965

Headlong, heedless, we rush
. . . to blast down the hills,
bulldoze the trees, scrape bare the fields
to build predestined slums . . . .
— NANCY NEWHALL
This Is the American Earth

Service interpreted its "multiple use" mandate as meaning, as McCloskey put it, "logging and something else." One of his first duties, among many others, was to help build support for Zahniser's Wilderness Act. Zahniser produced the first draft of his Wilderness Bill in 1956. That year the bill was introduced by Senator Hubert Humphrey of Minnesota and Congressman John P. Saylor of Pennsylvania. The struggle to build support for the bill would be a major preoccupation for the Club and other organizations over the next eight years.

Mike McCloskey was sent to build support for the bill in the home district of Congressman Wayne Aspinall of Colorado, by this time chairman of the House Interior Committee. McCloskey tells of arriving in Grand Junction with a colleague from the National Wildlife Federation. They took out a map, divided the district in half horizontally, rented two cars, and took off in opposite directions. McCloskey found a telephone book and looked up all the fishing and hunting guides and outfitters, hoping that they might tend toward supporting a wilderness act. Most did, and they agreed to sign telegrams to Aspinall urging his support for the bill. (At one point McCloskey approached the wrong packer and was threatened with being shot, but he managed to make a graceful enough exit and save his skin to fight another day.)

Over the next several years he organized support in Idaho and California as well. By 1964, with support for wilderness legislation strong and growing, Aspinall decided to allow the bill out of his committee and onto the House floor. He did not support the bill, but neither did he oppose it. He had won a concession that would allow mineral exploration and actual mining in wilderness areas until 1984—a bitter pill for the conservationists to swallow—and with this trade-off he was willing to allow the bill to become law. It was passed and signed by President Johnson on September 3, 1964. The process of designating inviolable wilderness areas on federal lands had begun.

WILDERNESS ON PAPER

The long struggle for a Wilderness Act had involved words and pictures, as virtually all conservation battles before and after have and will. A considerable benefit to the campaign, as well as a milestone in conservation publishing in its own right, was *This Is the American Earth* by Ansel Adams and Nancy Newhall, published in 1960.

This Is the American Earth grew out of a word-and-picture exhibit assembled for the Sierra Club's LeConte Lodge in Yosemite. As David Brower explains in his foreword, "The symbiosis [between Ansel Adams's camera and wilderness] went uninterrupted for some twenty-five years and led to this book's conception. The book was assisted when the National Park Service expressed a wish that something functional be done with the little building the Sierra Club had in Yosemite Valley as a memorial to Joseph LeConte, a pioneer conservationist. Ansel Adams suggested an exhibit of photographs and text that would combine to explain what national parks were really all about."[25] Adams asked Nancy Newhall to lend a hand with the text, having collaborated with her on books before and being an admirer of the exhibits she had mounted for the Museum of Modern Art in New York. Newhall wrote a powerful and poetic text lamenting humanity's transgressions against itself and against nature and making a stirring call for a change in the ways of society and civilization. One copy of the exhibit was displayed in Yosemite, another in San Francisco at the California Academy of Science. The Smithsonian Institution circulated it around the world.

The photographs were black and white, about half by Ansel Adams and half by other photographers. The masters of American black-and-white landscape photography were represented: Edward Weston, Minor White, Cedric Wright, Philip Hyde, Brett Weston, and Wynn Bullock, among others. Photojournalists were there as well, including Margaret Bourke-White and William Garnett. It was a powerful series of pictures, reinforced by Newhall's eloquent words. When David Brower looked at it, he knew it should be published. But how?

To do justice to an exhibition with photographs that were as much as several feet across, Brower, Adams, and Newhall needed a book that was big. They settled eventually on the size 10¼ × 13½″ and dubbed it "Exhibit Format." They added scenes from outside the United States photographed by Henri Cartier-Bresson, Ferenc Berko, and Werner Bischoff.

Finding a format was easier than finding a publisher, however. The book they had in mind would need to be printed on expensive paper to do justice to the photographs, and it would therefore have to be expensive: fifteen dollars, at a time when many art books sold for ten. All the publishers Brower approached feared that at that price they would be unable to sell enough copies to recoup their investment. That left only one solution: the Sierra Club must publish the book itself.

It took some doing to win the approval of the Club's Board of Directors for such an ambitious project, but eventually the Board agreed to take the plunge. *This Is the American Earth* was published by the Sierra Club in 1960. Review copies were sent to editorial-page editors as well as to critics. Supreme Court Justice William O. Douglas called it "one of the great statements in the history of conservation." Articles, editorials, and reviews appeared in scores of newspapers across the country. The Columbus, Ohio, *Citizen Journal* said, "No genius, with camera, brush, or pen, has done more to capture the natural beauty of this land." The Wichita, Kansas, *Beacon* said, "This book delivers the most important message of this century." Others praised it in the same vein. And despite the price, the book sold well, going through multiple printings in hardcover and then being brought back as a paperback a decade later. A new hardback edition was scheduled for publication in the fall of 1992; the pleasures of these images, and the pertinence of the message, are perennial.

The Sierra Club, which until then had published rather specialized titles—

George Ballis. Former Supreme Court Justice William O. Douglas, the high court's leading environmentalist, on a Club outing in the Sierra. c. 1961. Sierra Club Archives

OPPOSITE
In *This Is the American Earth*, 1960, Nancy Newhall asked: "Life and death on this planet now lie in Man's hands. . . . What are the forces of renewal? Only the source of life can tell us—only the living wilderness . . . where metamorphoses more strange than dreams call from the tadpole legs and from the dark worm in the chrysalis bright wings—where across oceans and hemispheres bird, fish and beast follow paths older than the continents. Are these mysteries we may penetrate or miracles we may only revere? The wilderness holds answers to more questions than we yet know how to ask."

Ansel Adams. Cedric Wright and Dorothy Mintz. 1927 High Trip to Kings Canyon National Park. © 1991 Trustees of the Ansel Adams Publishing Rights Trust. Wright, like his friend Ansel Adams, combined a love for music and a passion for photography. Ansel couldn't take his piano into the mountains; Cedric could take his violin, and he did, entertaining hundreds of Sierrans on the thirty-five High Trips he served as official photographer.

Cedric Wright. Suncups, a phenomenon of melting and freezing snow frequently encountered in the High Sierra in summer. c. 1950. Sierra Club Archives

Cedric Wright. Junipers at Timberline, Sawmill Pass. c. 1940. Sierra Club Archives

Cedric Wright. Ancient albicaulis (whitebark) pine, Sierra Nevada. c. 1947. Sierra Club Archives

WORDS
of the EARTH
C E D R I C   W R I G H T

Cedric Wright's *Words of the Earth*, with his text and photographs, was published in 1960, the second in the Exhibit Format series of books. There he wrote, "Melting snows, firm moist granite sand, fragrance of trees in the crystal air . . . these are the 'words of the earth,' so filled with quality that their mere existence is enough. There is a direct meaning in them — 'No argument, screaming, persuasion.' "

Patricia Caulfield. Left to right: Hugh Barnes of Barnes Press, David Brower, and Dr. Eliot Porter correct color proofs of *"In Wildness Is the Preservation of the World."* c. 1963. Sierra Club Archives

on mountaineering, backpacking, natural history, geology, and conferences — had burst into the popular book world.

Two more Exhibit Format books with black-and-white photographs were quickly published: first came *Words of the Earth* by Cedric Wright, a contemporary of Adams and a fixture on the High Trips. Wright was a tireless and talented photographer of the mountain scene, who entertained campers with his fiddle and loved to greet weary hikers at day's end with an unexpected cup of tea or soup. He provided both photographs and text for *Words of the Earth*, a mystical rumination on the meaning of nature and life. His book was followed by *These We Inherit: The Parklands of America* by Ansel Adams, a combined and expanded version of *My Camera in the National Parks* and *My Camera in Yosemite*.

In 1962 the Club's publishing program took another big, risky leap. Brower came across a physician-turned-photographer named Eliot Porter, born and reared in New England, a resident of New Mexico. Porter had put together color photographs of the New England wilderness with extracts from Henry David Thoreau's *Walden* and his voluminous journals. The photographs and the text reinforced each other, making the whole greater than the sum of the parts, as is the case with *This Is the American Earth* and all other Exhibit Format volumes. Joseph Wood Krutch, a naturalist and Thoreau scholar, pronounced Porter's selections superb and agreed to write a foreword to *"In Wildness Is the Preservation of the World."*

"In Wildness," with eighty pages of brilliant color pictures reproduced from Porter's four-by-five-inch transparencies, would have to cost not fifteen dollars but twenty-five dollars per copy. Again the Club decided to take the gamble, and again the gamble paid off. *"In Wildness"* outsold all its predecessors, going through many printings in hardcover, hundreds of thousands of copies in a smaller paperback edition. A "twenty-fifth anniversary edition" was published by the Sierra Club (just a little late) in 1989.

If Eliot Porter and Henry David Thoreau were made for each other, so were Richard Kauffman and John Muir. Porter and Thoreau represented the New England woods in symbiotic ways, ways not before seen; Kauffman provided color pictures of the High Sierra that illuminated Muir's text (drawn principally from *My First Summer in the Sierra* of 1911) in *Gentle Wilderness: The Sierra Nevada*.

It is hard to overestimate the importance of the Sierra Club's publishing program, both in the early sixties and subsequently. As a matter purely of bookmaking lore, the early Exhibit Format books are famous as pioneers of a style that would be widely imitated from then on, the combination of fine art with a political message, in a poetic juxtaposition that resonated for readers and viewers alike. In 1964, the entire Exhibit Format series was honored with the Carey Thomas Award — a coveted prize for excellence in book publishing — as the "Best example of creative publishing in the United States."

Publishing also introduced the Club to a vastly greater audience than it had theretofore reached, bringing thousands of new members into the organization. The Exhibit Format series — and the many other new and innovative

Eliot Porter. Spruce Trees in Fog and Hankweed, Great Spruce Head Island, Maine, July 1964

Eliot Porter. Wrecked Tree, Great Spruce Head Island, Maine, July 1964. These two photographs appeared in *Summer Island: Penobscot Country,* 1966.

"In Wildness Is the Preservation of the World"

SELECTIONS & PHOTOGRAPHS BY ELIOT PORTER

Eliot Porter trained as a physician and taught biochemistry and bacteriology at Harvard and Radcliffe before turning to photography full time in 1939. His preeminence as a nature photographer and a pioneer in color, which most critics had previously considered unsuitable to camera art, led to substantial monographs, many published by the Sierra Club, and exhibitions at The Metropolitan Museum of Art, The Museum of Modern Art, and other institutions. The photographs by Eliot Porter on this page and pp. 160–61 are reproduced by courtesy of the Eliot Porter Archives, Amon Carter Museum, Fort Worth, Texas.

Eliot Porter. Buttes at Sunrise near Rosarito, Baja California, August 1966. This and the photographs below and opposite top right were reproduced in *Baja California and the Geography of Hope* by Eliot Porter and Joseph Wood Krutch, an Exhibit Format book published in 1967.

BELOW
Eliot Porter. Idria Columnaria, Valley near Rosarito, Baja California, March 1964

OPPOSITE, CLOCKWISE
Eliot Porter. Espinosa Point, Galapagos, April 1966. Crabs and iguanas basking.

Eliot Porter. Morning Mist and Agave, Valley near Rosarito, Baja California, March 1964

Eliot Porter. El Pintudo and Scalesia, Santa Cruz, Galapagos, April 1966. This landscape and the two photographs to its left were published in Porter's two-volume *Galapagos*, 1968, in the Exhibit Format series.

Eliot Porter. Dead Mangrove and Lava, Espinosa Point, Galapagos, April 1966

160

Philip Hyde. Moonrise over Sharksnose and Shadow Lake, Wind River Range, Wyoming. n.d. Sierra Club Archives

Cedric Wright. Philip Hyde, a gifted and prolific photographer of the American wilderness for almost five decades, and a contributor to numerous Sierra Club publications, during a High Trip. c. 1950. Sierra Club Archives

FAR LEFT
Philip Hyde. Pass above Ardith Lake, Sawtooth Wilderness Area, Idaho. n.d. Sierra Club Archives

Philip Hyde, like Ansel Adams, Eliot Porter, and Cedric Wright, is a proponent of large-format photography, and he works with a 2¼″-square camera and a 4 x 5″ camera in both color and black and white. His special province is the desert Southwest, as seen in the illustrations on these two pages, from *Navajo Wildlands: As Long as the Rivers Shall Run*, an Exhibit Format book of 1967. They demonstrate Hyde's talent for composition and for capturing light and texture in that sometimes harsh, unforgiving landscape.

Philip Hyde. Ear of the Wind—Monument Valley Navajo Tribal Park, Arizona. 1964

ABOVE RIGHT
Philip Hyde. "Petrified" Sand Dunes at Canyon de Chelly National Monument, Arizona. 1966

Philip Hyde. Anasazi Pictographs at Standing Cow Ruin, Canyon de Chelly National Monument, Arizona. 1966

Philip Hyde. Totem Pole, Monument Valley, Arizona. 1964

BELOW LEFT
Philip Hyde. Granite Boulder and Boojum Tree, Baja, Mexico. 1981

Philip Hyde. Arch in Davis Gulch, Utah. 1964

styles and formats that followed—established the Sierra Club as the foremost conservation publisher in the country.

These early Exhibit Format books sold well, usually going through several printings and easily earning back the money invested in them. But they did not end the Club's need to pay attention to finances and find new routes to recruit new support. In another attempt to raise funds, Brower and Ian Ballantine of Ballantine Books hatched the idea of publishing calendars using the images from the books as illustrations. This innovation in publishing turned out to be a dazzling success, supporting the publications program and other Club enterprises. Since the 1970s the calendars have not used images from Club books exclusively but reproduce photographs from most of the country's leading free-lance landscape and wildlife photographers. The calendars too, like the Exhibit Format series that inspired them, became a widely imitated institution.

✺

THE LAST REDWOODS

Between 1962 and 1964 three books appeared in the Exhibit Format with a heightened combative tone and specific political objectives. The earliest was *The Last Redwoods* by Philip Hyde and François Leydet, an eloquent plea to Congress to create a Redwood National Park in Redwood Creek on the coast of Northern California.

By the 1960s most of the virgin redwood forests encountered by the first European settlers to reach the West Coast had been felled to build houses, boats, bridges, even to pave streets. National park status for various groves had been suggested beginning as early as the 1880s but had never come to pass, partly because of politics, mainly because the vast majority of national parks were carved out of land already owned by the federal government. Then the cost of creating any park was negligible—simply a change of management. This was not the case with the redwoods. To encourage railroad construction, the federal government had given away millions of acres of Western lands to privately owned railroad companies, which were encouraged to sell timber (or sell the land) to finance the opening of the West. By the time the push for a national park in the redwoods gained real momentum, it was clear that such a park would cost a very large sum of money indeed: the land was all privately owned and the trees standing on that land were extremely valuable.

By the mid-1960s, the Sierra Club was actively promoting creation of a Redwood National Park at Redwood Creek, a watershed containing the largest nearly undisturbed tract of old-growth redwoods still standing anywhere. As if ownership and acquisition were not a serious enough problem, a competing proposal was being advanced by the San Francisco-based Save-the-Redwoods League for a park in another site. The League, founded in 1919, had acquired many small groves of redwoods and donated them to the State of California for protection as state parks.

For the Redwood Creek campaign, the Club refined the full-page national newspaper advertisement as a major tactic. The first such ad had run in the *Denver Post* during the Dinosaur National Monument campaign. To save the redwoods, the Club placed an ad in *The New York Times*, the *Washington Post*, the *San Francisco Chronicle*, the *Los Angeles Times*, and the *Sacramento Bee*. It was written by Brower. Subsequent ads were produced in collaboration with the San Francisco ad agency, Freeman, Mander, and Gossage.

The first ad was an open letter to President Johnson, published on December 17, 1965, as "the last chance really to save the redwoods." It caused a sensation, since it both embarrassed the administration by accusing it of indecision and incensed the Save-the-Redwoods League by belittling that organization's park proposal. It also succeeded in its aim: to bring public attention to the controversy and build support for the Sierra Club's position. Conservation advertising was born, and it would be an integral part of most national environmental struggles over the next twenty-five years and beyond.

The redwood battle itself continued for many years. A park was established in 1968 in Northern California that combined the Club's and the League's proposals, weighted toward the former. But this left the Redwood National Park seriously vulnerable to logging on adjacent lands. A decade of litigation by the Sierra Club finally pushed Congress to acquire further acreage in 1978, to round out the park to its present dimensions.

TIME AND THE RIVER

As the controversy over saving the redwoods proceeded, another significant fight was gaining momentum: a proposal by the Bureau of Reclamation to build two dams within the greatest declivity on earth, the Grand Canyon.

Since the early 1950s, the state of Arizona had been working on a plan to provide water and power to Phoenix, Tucson, and other Arizona cities and towns whose growth potential seemed enormous. The scheme that the state and federal government hit on was to build a pair of dams in the Grand Canyon to provide salable electricity. The money would finance transmission lines and canals and other appurtenances; the electricity would be used to pump water not from either of the two reservoirs in the Grand Canyon, but from the Parker reservoir downstream. Same water, different source. Neither dam would be built within Grand Canyon National Park, but both would affect it severely. The upper reservoir would flood much of Marble Gorge above the park; the lower one, at Bridge Canyon, would back up forty miles into Grand Canyon National Monument, downstream from the park. A third project would divert up to ninety percent of the river's flow through a forty-mile tunnel, nearly drying up the stretch between reservoirs. The living river in the Grand Canyon would be replaced by two puddles, the riverbed between them would go nearly dry.

The Sierra Club had been caught uninformed and unprepared by the earlier proposal to drown Glen Canyon; not so the Grand Canyon. The Club

OVERLEAF

Gabriel Moulin. Old Redwood Highway. c. 1924. Moulin Studios, San Francisco The Sierra Club has been working to preserve redwoods since its founding, both the giant sequoia groves of the southern Sierra Nevada and the coast redwoods of northern California. The latter once covered two million acres in that region. Today ninety percent are gone. Some of the best of the remaining old-growth trees are protected in national and state parks, and conservationists are fighting to save the remnant still standing on private land. Sierra Club litigation has brought about the doubling in size of Redwood National Park and the cancellation or delay of many old-growth timber sales in the redwood region. Thanks to a successful Club campaign, logging within the redwood groves of Sequoia National Forest ended in 1990. In 1991 the Club is striving to have sequoias outside that park given firm statutory protection by the federal government.

ABOVE TOP
Harvey Richards. Logging in Humboldt
County, California. 1969. Sierra Club
Archives

ABOVE MIDDLE
Gabriel Moulin. Loggers and fallen
redwood, Humboldt County, California.
1920s. Moulin Studios, San Francisco

Anon. Coast redwoods preserved in
Redwood National Park, across the road
from clear-cut slopes. c. 1970. Sierra
Club Archives

Philip Hyde. Founder's Grove, Humboldt Redwoods State Park, California. 1977

Carr Clifton. Moss-covered Rhododendron, Emerald Ridge, California. 1988

BELOW
Kathleen Norris Cook. High Sierra from Bobcat Point, Sequoia National Park, California. 1980

OPPOSITE
Kathleen Norris Cook. Redwoods, Jedediah Smith State Park, Northern California. 1985

rolled into action. Seeing the early need to inform the public and its representatives of what was at stake, it created two books. The first, *The Place No One Knew: Glen Canyon on the Colorado*, was a requiem for Glen Canyon, then being drowned beneath Lake Powell. The color photographs were by Eliot Porter, the text from a variety of sources. More direct and topical was *Time and the River Flowing: Grand Canyon*, with a text by François Leydet. It was an unabashed polemic against the plan to dam the Colorado River inside the Grand Canyon. It too was illustrated with color photographs, but from several dozen photographers. A slide-film about Glen Canyon and the threats to the Grand Canyon was produced and circulated far and wide. A third book, *Grand Canyon of the Living Colorado*, was edited by the historian Roderick Nash (author of the seminal study *Wilderness and the American Mind*). Articles appeared in national magazines like *McCall's* and the *National Geographic*. The *Sierra Club Bulletin* covered the controversy extensively, as it did the parallel campaign for the redwoods.

Howard Gossage, his partner Jerry Mander, and Dave Brower then turned their attention to newspaper advertising, a series that would become the best known campaign for conservation in newspaper history and that according to many would turn the tide against the dams.

Four advertisements ran in the summer of 1966. The first was actually printed in two versions in a daily edition of *The New York Times*, the first time the newspaper had agreed to such an arrangement. Half the papers for that day carried one ad, half the other. The idea was to test the relatively quiet copy written by Brower against the harder-hitting version by Mander. Mander's outdrew Brower's by about three to two, as measured by the coupons soliciting donations to the Club that were clipped and returned to Club headquarters. Mander summed up the whole controversy: "Remember, with all the complexities of Washington politics and Arizona politics, and the ins and outs of committees and procedures, there is only one simple, incredible issue here: This time it's the Grand Canyon they want to flood. *The Grand Canyon.*"

The Club's redwoods advertisement may have made the administration uncomfortable, but its aim was basically to support a position the administration nominally favored. In the Grand Canyon it was different. Here the administration was pushing for the dams, and it would not tolerate such a broadside attack on its policy. The day after the ad ran, a representative from the Internal Revenue Service hand-delivered a letter to the Club's headquarters in San Francisco: it announced that the IRS was reviewing the Club's tax status and that from that day forward the agency could not guarantee (and therefore the Club could not guarantee) that contributions would be tax-deductible. The IRS's tentative ruling became final in 1969; litigation failed to have it reversed. Contributions to the Club since then have not been deductible as charitable contributions from the donor's income in determining taxes.

The federal government's desperate, heavy-handed tactic backfired in public opinion. The press got the story and blistered the IRS. Freedom of speech

ABOVE TOP
Kathleen Norris Cook. Grand Falls of the
Little Colorado River. 1985

ABOVE
Ruben Ruiz. Havasu Canyon,
Arizona. 1981

RIGHT
Philip Hyde. Yucca Blooms in Toroweap
Valley, Grand Canyon, Arizona. 1964

Philip Hyde. Aspens, North Rim, Grand
Canyon, Arizona. 1977

Kathleen Norris Cook. Descending
Clouds, West Rim of the Grand
Canyon, Arizona. 1981

Philip Hyde. Toroweap Overlook and the Colorado River, Grand Canyon National Park. 1964. Sierra Club Archives

ABOVE RIGHT
Martin Litton. Wooden dories are a traditional and, many claim, the best craft used to float the Colorado River in the Grand Canyon. 1960s. Sierra Club Archives

became an issue along with conservation. As Brower said later, "People who didn't know whether or not they loved the Grand Canyon knew whether they loved the IRS." Club membership soared—doubling from 39,000 to 78,000 in the three years following the IRS action. Large contributions dwindled but small ones grew fast, and some of the large ones were redirected to The Sierra Club Foundation, a tax-deductible entity created in 1960 as a hedge against just this sort of emergency.

And if the IRS meant to silence the Club on the matter of the Grand Canyon dams, it failed abysmally. Three more advertisements were run in quick succession, including the most famous of all, the "Sistine Chapel" ad. In reference to a Bureau of Reclamation suggestion that people in boats on the Grand Canyon reservoirs would enjoy motoring up close to the striped and sculptured canyon walls, the headline asked, "SHOULD WE ALSO FLOOD THE SISTINE CHAPEL SO TOURISTS CAN GET NEARER THE CEILING?"

Pressure on Congress and on the Interior Department mounted steadily, as an avalanche of letters poured in from across the country. Club chapters organized rallies and slide shows. Members gave speeches and showed films and slides to luncheon clubs and civic organizations. Student members recruited support on campuses. Finally, in the summer of 1967, the Bureau had to withdraw its proposal for dams in the Grand Canyon, because President Johnson had said he would veto any legislation with the dams in it. The next year Congress passed legislation authorizing a Central Arizona Project with a specific prohibition against any facilities within the Grand Canyon.

It was a great victory, the achievement of thousands of citizens inside and outside the Sierra Club, who wrote, sent telegrams, and placed telephone calls to their elected officials, filled the letters columns of daily papers with angry denunciations, and generally raised Cain.

But the Club and its allies did not have time to congratulate themselves for long; there was too much else to do as the 1960s drew to a close. The Forest Service had just approved plans for a monstrous ski resort in Mineral King in the Sierra Nevada that should by all rights have been included in Sequoia National Park. Club leaders were pressing for creation of a national park in the North Cascades in Washington. The battle for creation of a Redwood National Park was gaining a sort of desperate momentum as the lumber companies that owned the land cut as fast as they could before Congress could act to save the prime timberland.

Club members were busy across the country building public support for new reserves: at Point Reyes in California, Cape Cod in Massachusetts, Padre Island in Texas, the Oregon Dunes, and Fire Island in New York. The network of Sierra Club chapters by then covered most of the country. Local activists—many recruited and trained through the Grand Canyon affair—were turning their attention to matters closer to home, learning the techniques of influencing the decisions of state legislatures, city councils, and boards of selectmen.

჻

THE BATTLES WITHIN

Conservation activity was burgeoning everywhere in the United States in the 1960s. It brought with it an unwelcome but inevitable side effect: growing tensions within the Club itself. Some friction came from internal matters—the publications program, the relative authority and influence of members and chapters versus the professional staff, the extent to which decisions taken in one year could dictate the policies adopted subsequently—and some friction was generated by conservation policies and philosophies.

One prominent example of the latter set of problems drove a wedge between members of the board in the sixties and had one side accusing the other of conniving with greedy corporate interests. The centerpiece of the dispute was a plan by Northern California's Pacific Gas & Electric Company to build an installation of nuclear power plants on the central California coast. PG&E had its eye on the Nipomo Dunes near Santa Maria, a spot that had been suggested as appropriate for preservation as a state park. The Sierra Club urged the company to look elsewhere for a reactor site. PG&E responded diplomatically, saying in effect, "you help us identify an appropriate site and we'll try to use it if we can." People from the Club and the utility surveyed the countryside for a remote spot to build as many as seven giant nuclear plants. They needed to be remote in case of accident and they needed to be near the coast so that seawater could be used to cool the steam generated by the power plants.

At this time, the only concern over the proposed plants—or *any* nuclear plants—on the part of the Club and most other conservationists was where they were built. Whether or not to build the plants at all was hardly ques-

179

tioned in those days before the problems of nuclear waste management, reactor safety, and nuclear proliferation became evident to the public. Indeed, the Club had argued that the prospect of cheap, efficient nuclear power plants made the sacrifice of Dinosaur and Grand Canyon to hydroelectric dams unnecessary.

Eventually, PG&E suggested, and the Sierra Club endorsed, a plan to build the plants at Diablo Canyon at Point Buchon, due west of San Luis Obispo and north of Santa Barbara, on the last sizable, deserted stretch of central California coast. The Club put two conditions on its approval: that the problems of "thermal pollution" could be handled (the water returned to the ocean must not be so hot that it would damage the marine ecosystem), and that roads and power lines would interfere as little as possible with the scenery.

Surprisingly, given its usual staunch defense of roadless wild areas, the Club's board approved the site, although not one member of the board (except Martin Litton, who was abroad at the time) had ever seen Diablo Canyon. Several directors urged postponing the vote until a trip to the site could be made, but a majority preferred to approve the PG&E plan. The Club went on record as endorsing the Diablo site.

The matter was sufficiently contentious and the board so closely divided, however, that the decision was referred to a vote of the membership, a technique that had been used to ratify the board's policy on Hetch Hetchy. The board's Diablo Canyon action was endorsed by about seventy percent of the members voting.

It happened, however, that a board election coincided with this vote, and the composition of that body changed markedly. The new majority—some of whom by this time had visited the reactor site—opposed the siting of power plants there, and they rammed through a resolution withdrawing Sierra Club support for the plants. Directors from the old majority shouted "foul," arguing that the Club's credibility would be fatally damaged if it went back on its word. The new majority argued that the previous resolution had been a mistake, had been taken too hastily, and was in opposition to established Club policies concerning protection for wild and roadless areas, particularly on the coast.

The pro-Diablo, anti-reactor directors included Martin Litton, who had first enlisted as a Sierra Club activist during the Dinosaur controversy and had been a vocal leader in the Grand Canyon fight as well. He was scalding in his denunciations of the pro-reactor group and tireless in his campaign to save Diablo from PG&E. He was allied with Brower in this cause, though Brower was on staff, not a member of the board, and could not vote in matters before the directors. Leading the argument for the Diablo location were Ansel Adams, Dick Leonard, and William Siri, a biophysicist from Berkeley, a member of the first American team to scale Mount Everest's West Ridge, and a president of the Club in the mid-1960s. Publicly the Club seemed to vacillate on the Diablo Canyon question, while internally it struggled. Eventually, distracted with other organizational matters, it turned away

Martin Litton. The Diablo Canyon
nuclear power plant under construction
along a formerly pristine stretch of
central California coastline. 1970.
Sierra Club Archives

from the controversy altogether. Ultimately, two thousand-megawatt nuclear power plants were built on the shore of the Pacific Ocean at the mouth of Diablo Canyon.

OPPOSITE
Morley Baer. Forest Fog, Point Arena,
California. 1983

DISSATISFACTION WITH THE EXECUTIVE DIRECTOR

Diablo was only one element in a growing amount of deep-seated dissatisfaction with the performance of the executive director on the part of several members of the board of directors. Another matter of contention was the publications program, which was losing money, and which the anti-Brower faction, including his old friends Adams and Leonard, thought was taking too much of the organization's attention. Some of the books sold well and repaid their investment handsomely. Others did less well. And, indeed, financial success was not the only measure of a book's worth. *The Last Redwoods* sold out, but slowly, perhaps because so many of the photographs were stomach-churning scenes of ravaged hillsides and fields of stumps. After the first stage of the park battle was more or less won, books were less polemical. Later volumes examined subjects (Baja California, Big Sur, Maine's Penobscot Bay, Central Park, the Galapagos) that were less topical and less popular with the public. Fewer copies were bought. Brower shifted the argument, retorting that a substantial fraction of the Club's phenomenal membership growth could be attributed to the books, and he had surveys to prove it.

Brower believes most of the rancor of that period arose from publications policy and disagreements over Diablo Canyon. Other board members describe a broader set of problems, many having to do with the temperament of their executive director. By the late sixties, he had made enemies of some members of the board and also leaders of the volunteer membership — chapter leaders, for example, who thought the hired staff should spend more time and effort supporting local activities than Brower did.

It is the sort of conflict that visits many nonprofit, public-interest organizations. Opinions are strongly held; egos are large and fragile; strong leadership is resented by some, while strong leaders resent and resist attempts to control them. There were also matters of style in contention: how polite must the Sierra Club be in its dealings with the Forest Service, for example, or could the Club change its position on a project given the passage of time, or was a position once taken unchangeable?

On January 14, 1969, there was a shot heard round the Sierra Club world. It was an advertisement published in *The New York Times*. It covered a page and a half, and announced a new international series of Exhibit Format books that would "advance this urgent idea: an international program before it is too late, to preserve Earth as a conservation district' within the Universe, a sort of 'EARTH NATIONAL PARK.'" The ad had not been explicitly cleared by the Club president or the board. Brower said he was simply trying to promote Sierra Club publications and that no special permission was necessary. He was placed on a leave of absence, and he set about getting himself elected to the board of directors.

The campaign for the positions on the board was very public and very nasty. Ninety percent of the debate concerned Brower, who was accused of arrogance, insubordination, even fiscal mismanagement. He stoutly defended himself, but the chapters and their newsletters were mainly aligned with Brower's enemies and he had a difficult time getting his side of the dispute aired.

The San Francisco papers reported on the campaign at considerable length. Stories appeared in several national magazines, including *The Nation* ("Fratricide in the Sierra Club") and *Sports Illustrated* ("Brower Power Awaits the Verdict"). The national press was quite befuddled. Brower was by then one of the country's leading conservationists. John McPhee of the *The New Yorker* had spent the previous year working on a profile of Brower that would christen him the "Archdruid." What was all the ruckus about?

The election itself was conducted by mail ballot, as Sierra Club elections have been for many years. Brower and a supporting slate of candidates were trounced. There was nothing for him to do but resign as executive director.

The final act was played out in a large meeting room in the Sir Francis Drake Hotel in San Francisco on May 3, 1969. Fate had produced an extraordinary irony.

That morning's *San Francisco Chronicle* carried a front-page story reporting that the Wawona Tree—a giant sequoia in the southwestern part of Yosemite National Park with a tunnel cut through its base for carriages and, later, cars to pass through—had toppled and shattered sometime during the previous winter. Accompanying the story was a photograph of the tree in better days, with a Pierce-Arrow nosing into the tunnel and two or three people alongside. The picture had been taken by Ansel Adams. One of the people in the photograph was David Brower. The legend read "A Fallen Giant."

John McPhee, in his book about Brower titled *Encounters with the Archdruid*, reported the climax of the meeting as follows.

> The event of the day occurred in less time than it would take to tack a notice to a wall. President Wayburn recognized [William] Siri, and Siri said that David Brower was "the greatest spiritual conservation leader of this century." He added, "However, two giants are in conflict—the body of the Sierra Club and the embodiment of David Brower. I move that his resignation be accepted."
>
> Richard Leonard seconded the motion and was hissed as he did so.
>
> Perhaps incredibly, Brower, standing in the back of the room, still felt hopeful. There could be a change of heart.
>
> All in favor? Ten. Opposed? Five. Carried.
>
> In a soft, emotional voice, Brower read a farewell speech that contained no pumice. From its tone, he might have been reading a story to children around a campfire. Then he left the room.

Mike McCloskey was named interim chief of staff, soon elevated to executive director. Approximately a quarter of the staff, perhaps a dozen people, were dismissed or resigned in protest. A month later Brower became executive director of the John Muir Institute for Environmental Studies. Shortly thereafter he announced to the press the official formation of Friends of the Earth and pledged that the new organization would undertake the tasks the Sierra Club did not want him to tackle as its employee.

The new leadership of the Club—McCloskey, newly elected President Phillip Berry, an Oakland, California, lawyer who had learned conservation at Brower's knee—and the new board moved quickly to minimize any damage that might follow Brower's departure. They assured members that the Club's allegiance to bold conservation activity was undiminished, and invited chapter and group leaders to participate in the building of the new Club, where volunteers would once again play a leading role.

There was, under the circumstances, remarkably little rancor once Brower's resignation took effect. For all their differences over style, strategy, and tactics, the players were all devoted conservationists and would all return to working together soon, with no slackening of commitment or energy.

L A W S ,
L O B B Y I N G , A N D
L I T I G A T I O N

S H A R P E N I N G N E W S K I L L S ,
B R O A D E N I N G T H E A G E N D A ,
A N D S P R E A D I N G T H E W O R D
1 9 7 0 ⁊ 1 9 8 0

Carr Clifton. False Hellebore in Mineral King Basin, California. 1989

OPPOSITE
Carr Clifton. Old Cabin and Farewell Canyon in the Distance, Mineral King, California. 1988

By the summer of 1969, the Brower era had ended and the McCloskey era had begun. The latter would have a distinctly legalistic tone to it, in part because Mike McCloskey was trained as a lawyer and experienced as a lobbyist, partly because the Club had a vigorous and enthusiastic committee of volunteer lawyers. Another, more important reason was that the public, weary of the Vietnam War, was rapidly becoming concerned with environmental quality and, responding to that interest, Congress was preparing to pass a large number of new environmental laws very quickly. A vigilant Sierra Club would be needed to ensure that the laws, once passed, would subsequently be enforced.

The 1970s would see an eruption of public interest in environmental quality and the creation of dozens of new organizations, from local ecology centers to new national organizations, from Greenpeace and Friends of the Earth to the Natural Resources Defense Council and Environmental Action. These organizations—and the Sierra Club as well—would steadily widen the scope of their interests, to encompass energy and transportation policies and the pollution of air and water, and they would even begin to cast their gaze abroad. It is at this point, some historians suggest, that the "conservation" movement became the "environmental" movement, the latter being more encompassing. This did not mean that the Club would abandon its traditional role, however. Quite the contrary: it was during this period that the fight for the biggest wilderness prize of all—Alaska—would be played out.

⁊

M I N E R A L K I N G
A N D T H E L A W O F T H E L A N D

Having just come through the most difficult period in its history, the Club's new leaders wanted to prove to the quizzical that the organization would not, as David Brower's campaign literature had charged, "revert to its days as an organization of 'companions on the trail.'" The new president, Phillip Berry,

the Oakland attorney, and the new executive director, Mike McCloskey, pounced immediately upon a proposal by the Walt Disney organization for a large ski resort on Forest Service land in the southern Sierra Nevada; it was, they thought, just the kind of fight the Club should take on, partly because of the resource involved and partly to prove that the Club retained its protectionist fervor.

In the late forties, the Club had said it would not object to a ski resort in Mineral King, a cul-de-sac on the southern edge of Sequoia National Park, about 250 miles from San Francisco. What the club would not object to was a small resort, however, and when the Forest Service invited would-be developers to bid on the project back then, none did. The idea was shelved and, momentarily, forgotten. Nearly twenty years later, Walt Disney stepped forward with a new proposal.

The Club and Disney were unlikely adversaries. In addition to his animated films, Disney had produced a series of wildlife movies that encouraged appreciation of animals and their habitat. The Sierra Club made Disney an honorary life member in 1956.

In addition to animals, in two and three dimensions, Walt Disney had at least one other passion, and it was skiing. In the middle sixties, his representatives quietly asked the Forest Service if it would entertain a new proposal for a ski resort at Mineral King, and the agency said it would. Disney had his agents begin inquiring about whether the "inholdings"—parcels of private acreage surrounded by Forest Service land—in and near Mineral King were for sale.

It was all done very discreetly, but rumors of the maneuvering found their way to a Sierra Club member named John Harper, a geologist from Bakersfield who served on the Club's local chapter conservation committee. Harper began writing letters, both to the Forest Service to find out what was going on and to San Francisco to alert Club headquarters and enlist its support. Harper and his colleagues began a series of visits to Mineral King to catalogue the resources at stake there.

In February 1965 the Forest Service advertised for developers and got six bids, two of which it considered serious. It chose Disney as the developer. The Forest Service had foreseen a modest development, but the Disney proposal was hardly that. It included twenty-seven lifts and a ten-story parking lot, plus a laundry, chapel, restaurants, hotels, and even dams across the valley's creeks to keep debris from washing down the hillsides. There would be accommodation for three thousand overnight guests and one thousand employees. Daytime would see as many as fourteen thousand people frolicking in the snow. Disney wanted Mineral King to challenge Sun Valley and Chamonix as a world-class ski resort.

The main problems with this scheme were that Mineral King is too small for such an extensive development, its slopes are terribly prone to avalanches, and it is twenty-five miles from a paved road. The road that does reach the valley is open only from June to October, depending on snow, and it would have to be realigned and regraded to permit snowplows to keep it accessible

Cedric Wright. Phillip Berry on a High Trip, 1950s. Sierra Club Archives. The Stanford-trained lawyer Phil Berry helped create the Sierra Club Legal Defense Fund in 1971, and he served as Club president from 1969 to 1971. His wife, Michele Perrault, was also president of the Club, in 1984–86. She has led resistance to drilling for oil off the Northern California coast and has chaired the Club's International Committee. (Three other couples have been Club directors: Ansel and Virginia Adams, Edward and Harriet Parsons, and Francis and Marjorie Farquhar.)

during winter. This was not the simple rustic resort the Club had accepted in principle in 1949. After considerable internal debate about the Club's going back on its word, the directors decided to oppose the Disney proposal with all their might.

McCloskey asked the Forest Service to hold a public hearing on the resort proposal. But the Forest Service said there had been a public meeting to discuss Mineral King in 1953 and that was good enough. The State of California, Ronald Reagan presiding, said it would provide the first of the considerable sums required to fix the road, and surveying began. In an unofficial response, Martin Litton, a member of the Club's board from 1964 to 1972, recruited busloads of students who made a weekly trek to remove survey stakes for the road into Mineral King. This was not a Club-sponsored protest, but Club members took part. Stewart Udall, Secretary of the Interior for both presidents Kennedy and Johnson, did his best to block the project, but he eventually relented and granted permission for the road to be upgraded where it crossed the finger of Sequoia National Park that separated Mineral King from the outside world. The only place left for the Club to turn to was federal court.

McCloskey had already begun to explore the possibilities of challenging the Disney plan legally. It would be a bold step, not quite unprecedented, but nearly so. Until 1966, conservationists had been regularly tossed out of court since they could not demonstrate a financial interest in the projects they were challenging or the resources they were trying to defend. They were deemed to lack what is known as "standing to sue."

In 1966 the Scenic Hudson Preservation Conference, with some assistance from the Club, had gained a landmark ruling from the Second Circuit Court of Appeals that it could successfully assert standing in proceedings concerning the Storm King hydroelectric project in upstate New York. The Conference was entitled to standing, the court ruled, owing to its "aesthetic, conservational or recreational" interest in the place.

In June 1969, the Sierra Club filed suit against the Forest Service in federal district court in San Francisco. It asserted three causes of action. First, it was contrary to Park Service policy to permit construction of a road that was not being built to provide access to the park itself. Second, the leases that the Forest Service wanted to grant Disney comprised more acres and ran longer than Forest Service regulations allowed. Third, Mineral King was technically a "game reserve," and game reserves were hardly compatible with mammoth ski resorts.

In addition to saving Mineral King, the Club was trying to broaden the standing doctrine rather dramatically. The Hudson River organization had acquired standing to participate in a federal agency's hearings; the Sierra Club wanted standing to challenge an agency's action in federal court.

Judge William Sweigert, a close associate of Earl Warren when he was governor of California, read the briefs, listened to some hours of argument, and produced the injunction the Sierra Club had asked for. The Forest Service was forbidden to issue the permit to Disney until the court had an opportunity to explore the principles at stake in a trial.

The Forest Service, hoping for a quick victory, asked the Court of Appeals to dismiss the suit on the grounds of the Sierra Club's lack of standing. If it prevailed, it might forever close the courthouse door to conservation organizations and others that wanted to challenge its decisions — and its judgment — in court.

On the vital issue of standing, the Club decided to try for the brass ring. It could have argued that its members used Mineral King for hiking, fishing, and camping; it could have pointed out all the Sierra Club outings that had passed through Mineral King over the years. Rather, it chose to argue that it should have standing to sue simply because it was the Sierra Club and that its whole *raison d'être* was to do battle for places like Mineral King.

But this was too long a stretch for the Court of Appeals. It threw the case out of court. The Club asked the Supreme Court to review the decision, and the high court agreed to do so.

The Supreme Court's ruling in the case has been called a defeat, a victory, and several things in between. The Court said that, based on the way the Sierra Club had presented its case, it did not have the requisite standing. It also said, however, that if the Club would revise its pleadings to indicate how its interests and the interests of its members would be damaged by the ski resort, the Club would qualify to argue its case in court.

The Club revised its papers, the injunction was reimposed, and the Forest Service set about to reassess the projected impact of the project on the valley. The fight for Mineral King moved from the legal back to the political arena.

Sierra Club members, led by John Harper and Martin Litton, among others, staged hike-ins to Mineral King, wrote letters-to-the-editor, distributed films, sent out press releases, cajoled politicians, and stimulated articles in national magazines and newspapers. Public support for the project soon faded, along with political support and the interest of the Disney organization. By the time the Forest Service's study was finished in 1975, the Disney people had given up. In 1978 Congress made Mineral King a part of Sequoia National Park.

THE SIERRA CLUB LEGAL DEFENSE FUND

In his speech to the Sierra Club's first annual meeting, held in 1895, John Muir called the serious business of the organization "lawyer's work." Lawyers had been prominent in Club affairs since the organization was born in a lawyer's office in 1892, but they had not actually taken conservation issues to court until the 1960s. Then, the Club's volunteer legal committee, led by Donald Harris, Fred Fisher, and Phil Berry, began representing the Club in appeals of timber sales and dam permits. Litigation was filed against numerous developers and other commercial interests, mainly around San Francisco Bay. When the time came to work up a suit concerning Mineral King, it was clear none of the volunteer lawyers could take on such a major case in

Anon. Martin Litton, a Club leader since the 1950s and a photographer who documented many of its battles, joins Sierra Club rock climbers at a practice climb in southern California. c. 1951. Photograph taken with Litton's camera by one of the climbers. Sierra Club Archives

his or her spare time. They began to think that a well-funded, full-time litigation organization might be a worthwhile idea to investigate.

And so, when the Club took the Mineral King case back to Judge Sweigert of the federal district court in San Francisco, the lawyer for the plaintiff was James Moorman, a young man from North Carolina. Moorman had joined the Club after happening upon its Exhibit Format series of books, and he had helped found the Southeast (now Potomac) Chapter in Washington, D.C. In 1971, through the efforts of Berry, Harris, Fisher, and Mike McCloskey, and with the support of the Ford Foundation, the Sierra Club Legal Defense Fund was created. Moorman was its first executive director.

The Legal Defense Fund was established as legally independent of the Club, with its own board of trustees (an overwhelming majority of whom were lawyers), its own staff, its own budget, and its own offices. It applied for and was granted tax-deductible status by the Internal Revenue Service, since it did not anticipate lobbying or pursuing other activities to influence pending legislation, which is what the IRS accused the Club of doing too vigorously when the Service removed the tax-deductibility of contributions to the Club in 1966.

The establishment of the Legal Defense Fund came at a time that some analysts have identified as a move by environmental organizations to a new professionalism. The Sierra Club was setting up a law firm to litigate cases for itself and others. The Club itself began to develop a staff of professionals trained and experienced in their jobs and to move away from hiring passionate amateurs. The Environmental Defense Fund had just been formed, the creation of biologists worried about the deleterious effects of pesticides, among other concerns. And the Natural Resources Defense Council, also seeded by a grant from the Ford Foundation, was created during this period by a group of young Yale Law School graduates. EDF and NRDC would become dual law-and-science organizations; the Sierra Club Legal Defense Fund would stick to litigation. The three would compete for funding but work together closely on matters of law and public policy.

The Legal Defense Fund, along with the other two organizations, grew swiftly. A Denver office of the Legal Defense Fund opened in 1972. Offices in Washington, D.C., and Juneau opened in 1978. By the time of the Legal Defense Fund's twentieth anniversary in 1991, there were offices in eight cities and a staff of thirty-five attorneys, litigating dozens of cases on a wide variety of topics.

A D M I R A L T Y   I S L A N D , T H E   F O R T R E S S   O F   T H E   B E A R S

Along with Mineral King, another case the Legal Defense Fund inherited from the past involved Admiralty Island in southeast Alaska, which was only the first skirmish in what would be the Club's major public-lands focus for the 1970s: the struggle for the wilderness that constituted most of the forty-ninth

Carr Clifton. Two views of the mountains of Admiralty Island, Alaska. Both 1988. Alaska has been the scene of several classic conservation confrontations—over Admiralty Island, the trans-Alaska pipeline, the hunting of the bowhead whale, and the creation of millions of national parks and wildlife refuges. At the end of the 1980s Big Oil attempted to open the Arctic National Wildlife Refuge to exploration and exploitation of its possible petroleum deposits. Then the *Exxon Valdez* went on the rocks and the refuge was spared, at least for a time. America's continuing overreliance on oil and the insecurity of foreign supplies, however, ensure another attack some time on the refuge—and on any other place in the state, and on the globe, thought to have petroleum underfoot. If Gary, Indiana, epitomizes what has gone wrong with American industrial civilization, Alaska represents what is still left to save.

Robert Glenn Ketchum. Finger Mountain and the Finger River Estuary, Hoonah Sound, Alaska. 1985

state. Alaska was, as the Club's Bob Waldrop wryly noted, "The last chance to do it right the first time." At Admiralty, the Forest Service seemed hell-bent on doing it as wrong as conceivably possible.

Admiralty lies just offshore Juneau, a long, narrow, million-acre island that is home to the world's greatest concentrations of bald eagles and Alaskan brown bears — better known as grizzlies. It is also home to deer and several species of fur-bearing animals, and it hosts five separate species of salmon as they spawn in the island's sixty-seven salmon streams. Admiralty is also the site of a magnificent forest of hemlock and spruce, part of the Tongass National Forest. Thence arose the problem.

The historical mission of the Forest Service was to manage the national forests for various purposes, with timber production, protection of water-sheds and wildlife habitat, and support for recreation principal among them. That mandate left ample room for argument, and argument there was, over the importance the agency gave to timber production for the most part, particularly in the years following World War II. In southeast Alaska, the problem intensified when the Forest Service took on the role of economic development agent and set out to turn millions of acres of virgin forest into jobs and dollars.

The agency looked around and saw the Tongass National Forest, an extra-ordinary forest of ancient, giant trees that covers sixteen million acres, virtu-

192

Robert Glenn Ketchum. Lichens and Moss on the Shore of an Alpine Lake, Misty Fjords National Monument, Alaska. 1987

Art Wolfe. Rain Forest, Brothers Island, Southeast Alaska. 1986. In this, one of the few largely intact rain forests in the world's temperate zone, carpets of moss muffle the sound of nearby ocean surf.

ally all the Alaskan panhandle. The trees were in a "climax forest"—"old growth" to their admirers, "overmature" to the Forest Service. Official Forest Service policy, then as now, was to liquidate old-growth forest in the Tongass and let young, faster-growing trees replace it.

Edgar Wayburn, Club president in 1964–67 and again in 1969–70, and his wife, Peggy, had begun a lifelong romance with Alaska on a visit in 1967. The visit was not only their first, it was also the first official visit by an officer of the Sierra Club to Alaska. They were following in the footsteps of John Muir, who had made trips during his non-writing days—in 1879, 1880, and 1890—to Southeast and had spent a few nights camped on Admiralty's shore. Teddy Roosevelt had suggested setting Admiralty aside as a bear sanctuary in 1901; the Club had nominated it for a national park in the 1930s, yet it remained unprotected.

In addition to these historical connections with the Club, Admiralty Island has wildlife in a profusion unmatched anywhere in North America. The Club's leadership realized that if ever an organization and a state were made for each other, they were the Sierra Club and Alaska.

What Wayburn did not know on his 1967 visit, because the Forest Service had made no public announcement of the news, was that the forest on Admiralty Island was slated for razing. The Forest Service was determined to sell off Admiralty's timber. Two contracts had been signed and cancelled. In 1967 the agency was trying to interest U.S. Plywood; in 1968 the agreement was signed. It gave the company the right to log nearly nine billion board-feet of timber on Admiralty: over a period of fifty years it could cut down every mature tree on the island. It was the biggest single timber contract that the Forest Service had ever entered into.

Protests were proffered, appeals were launched. U.S. Plywood insisted that it would do everything necessary to protect the wildlife resources of the island. The company went so far as to empanel a committee of distinguished ecologists to advise it on how to proceed, how to build a mill and log a forest without causing unacceptable amounts of damage.

The Sierra Club and local sportsmen and conservationists viewed the blue-ribbon panel with extreme skepticism. Its chairman, A. Starker Leopold of the University of California at Berkeley, was one of the most highly regarded wildlife biologists of his time and the son of Aldo Leopold, founder of The Wilderness Society. Why would Starker accept an appointment from a timber company, giving respectability to the company's logging plans? When the ecologists' panel was introduced to the press and the public at the old Baranof Hotel in Juneau, conservationists heckled the speakers. Starker Leopold tried to assure them that he would run an objective investigation.

Unwilling to await the results of the Leopold study, the Sierra Club and a few other organizations filed suit, claiming that the logging plan was contrary to the Forest Service's governing law, that the logging would decimate the island's wildlife, and that the agency's economic analysis of the whole situation was faulty. Tempers were high and rising when the trial was held in Juneau in 1970. The marquee of the motel between the airport and the town

Anon. Edgar and Peggy Wayburn. 1948. Sierra Club Archives. Peggy Wayburn has written scores of articles for the *Sierra Club Bulletin* and a dozen books on subjects as far-flung as Alaska and the Florida wetlands. Ed is in his twenty-ninth year as a Club director and was president for two terms. Together, they have led campaigns to preserve Alaska—the wildest of the wild—and to create the Golden Gate National Recreation Area—near their home in San Francisco.

OPPOSITE
Carr Clifton. Low Tide, Gambier Bay, Admiralty Island National Monument, Alaska. 1989

said "Sierra Club Go Home!" The children of conservationists fought the children of pro-logging residents during recess at school.

A parade of witnesses held forth on the results of logging carried out in earlier days, on a small scale, on Admiralty and nearby. They spoke of hillsides that slumped into the crystal streams, of ruined salmon runs. They begged the court to spare the magnificent island, but the court remained unimpressed. The Forest Service was adjudged to be well within its rights to make a contract with the company, which had been acquired by Champion International and was now known as Plywood-Champion. The Club appealed.

Before the Court of Appeals had time to render a decision, the Leopold Commission's report was released. It found that the logging as contemplated by the Forest Service would indeed wipe out Admiralty's wildlife. The hardest-hit species would be the Sitka black-tailed deer, a staple food of the Tlingit Indians who occupied Angoon, the only permanent settlement on the island.

Native Americans had been the accidental victims of much environmental abuse for two centuries, to say nothing of the deliberate abuse they suffered at the hands of European settlers. Frequently the interests of natives and of conservationists coincided. The struggle for Admiralty Island was clearly one such case. Where the plaintiffs in the original suit were conservation groups and a hunting guide, subsequent litigation found the residents of Angoon on the court papers as well, both collectively and individually. Following release of the Leopold report, the Club's and the Native Americans' lawyers from the Legal Defense Fund persuaded the Court of Appeals to suspend consideration of the case and remand it to the District Court with instructions to reopen proceedings to consider this new evidence. The new evidence was duly presented, and the judge took the case under advisement. He never ruled: more than a year later Plywood-Champion decided the fight was not worth the trouble and canceled its agreement with the Forest Service, forfeiting its $100,000 deposit. Following vigorous lobbying by Club members and others in Juneau and elsewhere, and by the Club's leadership and staff led by Ed Wayburn, most of the island was proclaimed the Admiralty Island Wilderness National Monument in 1977 and retained under management of the Forest Service.

❧

EARTH DAY, 1970: THE ENVIRONMENTAL MOVEMENT IS BORN

By the spring of 1970, public interest in environmental protection was surging. In part, it was the simple incremental growth of concern for a planet under increasing pressure. It also grew out of the public's disillusionment with the war in Vietnam and its perennial search for a cause to believe in and work for. Most important was probably the landing of a manned spacecraft on the moon in the summer of 1969 and the unforgettable photographs of the earth the astronauts brought back with them. The sight of the fragile, vulnerable blue ball floating in black space — the only living thing we know for certain exists in the universe — made millions of people stop and think about what humanity was doing to its home.

Reacting to this wider focus of concern, on January 1, 1970, President Nixon signed into law the National Environmental Policy Act, a formal response by the federal government to the public demand for action, as evidenced by rallies and protests across the country. NEPA, innocuous on the surface, requires environmental impact studies of all major projects built on federal land or with federal funds and an investigation of alternatives to each particular project. It would be the cornerstone of conservationists' action — both at the grassroots and in the courtroom — from then on.

April 22, 1970, had been declared Earth Day by a group headed by Senator Gaylord Nelson of Wisconsin and Congressman Pete McCloskey of California (no relation to Mike). It was described as "The first national environmental teach-in," and it brought together millions of people at parades, conferences, fairs, and picnics in parks and on campuses in many places. As part of its contribution to Earth Day, the Sierra Club produced a mass-market paperback book that sold four hundred thousand copies. Titled *Ecotactics*, it was an anthology of ideas and strategies for getting involved in environmental action. *The Environmental Handbook*, from Friends of the Earth, was similarly aimed and sold a million copies. The public was ready not only to read about what the newspapers loved to call the "environmental crisis" but also to *do* something about it — by writing letters, attending meetings, lobbying public officials, and altering their behavior with respect to consumption (recycle more), travel (drive less), and other matters.

In October 1969 the Club's conservation department had launched the weekly *National News Report* to keep volunteer leaders informed, via first-class mail, of important developments in Congress and the executive agencies. Copies of the *NNR* published during the early seventies and later show a lively diversity of stories, and nearly as wide a diversity in the subject matter involving Club activists. During the 1970s Club activists were hard at work to establish new national parks or other reserves at Canyonlands and Capitol Reef in Utah, Apostle Island in Wisconsin, the Big Thicket in Texas, and Sleeping Bear Dunes in Michigan. They were busily (and successfully) blocking the Cross-Florida Barge Canal, the High Ross Dam in the North Cascades in Washington, dams on the Snake River in Hells Canyon on the Idaho/Oregon border, and a housing development in a sensitive habitat in Hawaii. They were already working to ensure a reliable supply of fresh water to the Everglades and the Big Cypress Swamp, a struggle that continues to this day. They were resisting the overuse of herbicides on public land in New Mexico, among other states. They were stopping the building of roads in inappropriate places such as the Joyce Kilmer National Forest in North Carolina.

Carr Clifton. Sunrise Reflects in Water Tanks, Canyonlands National Park, Utah. 1988. The subject of much Club lobbying in the late 1950s, Canyonlands won National Park designation in 1964. Monument Basin, below, is in Canyonlands; the "water tanks" seen at left are natural basins.

Carr Clifton. Junction Butte and Sandstone Formations in Monument Basin, Utah. 1989

OPPOSITE
John Ward. Reflection of Angel Arch, Canyonlands National Park, Utah. 1980

Carr Clifton. Grass and Canyon Rim
above Soda Springs Basin, Utah. 1988

Carr Clifton. Sunset, Big Cypress National Preserve, Florida. 1989

Ted Schiffman / Peter Arnold, Inc. The Highly Endangered Florida Panther, Everglades, Florida. c. 1981

OPPOSITE
Carr Clifton. Sawgrass and Cypress, Big Cypress National Preserve, Florida. 1989. These three photographs show the wilderness that survives at the tip of Florida. In the past few decades, agricultural and residential development has altered the natural flow of the waters that sustain the Everglades and has polluted much of what still flows into the famed "River of Grass." The result has been the invasion of exotic species of plants that choke off native flora and tiny fauna and disastrous fires that destroy large tracts and smudge the skies for miles around.

Anon. Oil-soaked waterfowl after a tanker spill off the New England coast. U.S. Fish and Wildlife Service

The foregoing speaks mostly of disagreements over how to manage public lands and public resources, which is a reasonable description of the focus of the Club's conservation work throughout its history. In the early 1970s, much environmental debate also seemed to swirl around energy, both as a matter of public policy and in specific projects proposed to extract specific fuels from the earth.

One event that ignited the public's interest in energy resources, and led to a questioning of how the country takes and uses various fuels, came in the spring of 1969 when the Union Oil Company's Platform A in the Santa Barbara Channel off Southern California had a disastrous blowout, fouling beaches with crude oil and killing uncounted thousands of birds. The Sierra Club dispatched a group of young staff members from San Francisco, who joined Club members in Santa Barbara immediately following the spill, and together they monitored the clean-up and fought with the oil company and government officials over proposals to spray cosmetic but toxic dispersants on the slick to dissipate bad publicity. They had learned from the *Torrey Canyon* accident off the southwest coast of England a few years before, which had fouled Channel beaches; dispersants sprayed on the oiled beaches were thought to have increased the harm done to the wildlife. Few dispersants were used at Santa Barbara.

Not long after the blowout at Platform A, two tankers operated by the Standard Oil Company of California collided beneath the Golden Gate Bridge, spilling massive amounts of oil, which blackened beaches and killed wildlife both inside the Bay and outside on the ocean coast. The Club helped mobilize volunteer clean-up crews and made sure the company and the government pursued restoration of the damage as vigorously as possible.

Oil, even when it did not spill, had become one of the main points of environmental contention by the beginning of the 1970s. At that time, the biggest and most controversial energy project was the Trans- Alaska Pipeline, put forward by a consortium of oil companies and the U.S. government.

The Trans-Alaska Pipeline would transport oil from beneath the North Slope of Alaska to the port of Valdez via a forty-eight-inch-diameter, eight hundred-mile-long pipe through the wildest country left in America. The Sierra Club and many other conservation organizations objected to the project for a variety of reasons, including the violation of the vast Alaskan wilderness, the danger to wildlife and watersheds along the pipeline, and the possibility of a calamitous spill from a tanker in Prince William Sound. The environmentalists fought the proposal valiantly in Congress and the courts and delayed it for several years. The project that was built is much safer than it otherwise would have been, but in 1990 it was already in need of maintenance and replacement estimated to cost more than $3 billion.

As discussed in chapter three, the Sierra Club's first intimate brush with nuclear power had been at Diablo Canyon in California, where the Club's objections to the project were confined to its site. A more fundamental concern was growing with the technology itself, however, both with respect to safety and the disposal of the extremely hazardous waste that remains when nuclear fuel is used up. Club activists had helped to fend off a proposal by the Atomic Energy Commission to bury high-level radioactive waste from the nation's commercial nuclear power plants under wheat fields at Lyons, Kansas in the early 1970s, and many members were coming to question the technology itself. Scientists from the University of California and the Massachusetts Institute of Technology had begun to release studies that suggested the danger from reactors was many times more serious than the government would admit. In 1974, responding to these studies, the Club called for a moratorium on the construction of new nuclear power plants pending resolution of these and other problems. At this writing, the political disorder in the Mideast following the Gulf War, coupled with increased concern about global warming, has incited renewed calls for "a new generation of safe nuclear power plants." The calls, according to most experts, are likely to fall on deaf ears. Even if the safety of nuclear plants could be assured, they remain a thoroughly uneconomic means of generating electricity, far more expensive than other methods. The problem of waste disposal and monitoring for hundreds of thousands of years remains to be solved.

Debate about energy policy in 1990 in many respects replayed that triggered by the oil crisis of 1973, when the members of OPEC — the Organization of Petroleum Exporting Countries, which includes the oil producers of the Middle East and Africa plus Venezuela, Ecuador, and Indonesia — shut off the oil supply to the West. Long gas lines formed, political panic set in, and Congress voted to bar further legal challenges to the operation of the Alaska pipeline. By the late seventies, when a second OPEC embargo was announced, Jimmy Carter's presidency was in trouble. He made his famous retreat to Camp David where he found America plunged into a deep "malaise" and determined that the energy crisis was a big part of the reason. He announced a campaign to defeat the malaise — "the moral equivalent of war," he called it — which was breeding headlines and confusion.

To best the beast, Carter proposed an Energy Mobilization Board (EMB) with powers to exempt energy projects (nuclear and coal power plants and the like) from environmental laws. He proposed a Synthetic Fuels Corporation (SFC) to spend as much as $88 billion to subsidize the efforts of private companies to produce liquid fuel from oil shale, tar sands, corn stalks, and other exotic materials. The problem was not that such fuels could not produce usable energy; they could. The problem was the cost, both economic and environmental. A better investment, conservationists argued, would be in efficiency and in the renewable sources — solar, wind, geothermal. It took all the energy the environmental movement could muster, along with stout resistance from conservative politicians who did not like spending such gigantic sums on anything, particularly underwriting private enterprises, but the EMB was stopped. The SFC began but was killed a few years later.

BANNING THE BOOM

An unusual battle in the seventies for the Sierra Club and other conservation organizations concerned an ongoing program by the federal government to underwrite an effort by the Boeing Company of Seattle to produce a commercial supersonic passenger airplane. It seemed at first only peripherally an environmental issue. Objections voiced by the conservationists, led by the Sierra Club and Friends of the Earth (the organization launched by David Brower after he resigned from the Club), were to the sonic booms that crash along the ground in the wake of an aircraft traveling at supersonic speed, the damage to the ozone in the upper atmosphere that protects surface dwellers on earth from harmful solar radiation, the fuel efficiency of the engines, and the lavish use of public funds to subsidize private industry. The environmentalists, building on lessons learned during the congressional fight over the Grand Canyon dams, organized a formidable "Coalition Against the SST," and began providing information and advice to activists across the country, Sierra Club chapter leaders and members prominent among them. These people, using arguments tailored to the particular interests of their legislators, persuaded members of Congress to oppose the SST project, and after a long battle it was defeated. To this day the United States manufactures no commercial supersonic aircraft; the French/English counterpart, the Concorde, has been so uneconomical that, unless an unforeseen technological breakthrough is made, the service will be phased out as the planes are retired.

KEEPING THE AIR INVISIBLE

Another nearly constant legislative struggle of the 1970s and beyond—one that occupied both volunteer members of the Club and the organization's staff and board and still does—was the attempt to clean up dirty air and to protect clean air. Congress passed the Clean Air Act in 1970. It laid out a series of schedules and deadlines for the Environmental Protection Agency for meeting goals with respect to different classifications of pollutants—carbon monoxide, sulfur dioxide, particulates, and so on. For most pollutants the deadline was 1977. For most, the deadlines were missed, and a mountain of litigation by environmentalists was necessary to keep the EPA and state air-pollution agencies remotely near the schedule that Congress had decreed. One chapter of the clean air story is particularly interesting.

Earlier federal air pollution law and regulations had encouraged the "prevention of significant deterioration" of air quality. The name for this effort was shortened to PSD, and it came to signify efforts to protect clean-air areas, particularly in the Southwest, from the new coal-fired power plants then being proposed by local and regional utilities to serve the growing communities both nearby and as far away as Nevada and California. In the early 1970s, however, when the Environmental Protection Agency, established by presidential decree in 1970, proposed regulations to implement the Clean Air Act, the idea of PSD was nowhere to be found, having been replaced by proposed rules that would have allowed considerable pollution of those pristine skies. The Sierra Club could imagine the nation's beloved Grand Canyon disappearing under a blanket of yellow-brown smog. It filed suit.

The suit turned on three words in the 1970 act, the ones that said the purpose of the law was to "protect and enhance" air quality. That has to mean, the lawyers argued, that existing air quality must not be allowed to deteriorate. The courts agreed, all the way to the Supreme Court, and Congress wrote PSD explicitly into the law when amendments were adopted in 1977. It is now illegal for an agency to allow the deterioration of air quality over "Class One" areas: national parks, wilderness areas, and so forth. This provision has helped discourage construction of a number of power plants that would have sullied the skies over many Western parks and other open areas.

❧

UNFINISHED BUSINESS IN THE PARKS

Notwithstanding its success protecting the air, the Club's principal interest was still public lands, and there was much unfinished business as the Carter administration took office in January 1977. Carter had been elected with strong support by conservationists owing to his record as Georgia governor and his policy statements during the presidential campaign. Richard Nixon, despite his signing the National Environmental Policy Act and many other strong environmental laws, and despite his creating the Environmental Protection Agency, had been on the opposite side of the Sierra Club on most environmental disputes. So had Gerald Ford. Conservationists had high hopes for the new Carter administration, particularly when it tapped high-level staff members from a number of environmental organizations to serve in government.

One of the hoary items on the Sierra Club's agenda was "rounding out" the national park system. New parks were needed in many places, as park-caliber lands came under pressure from developers, and many existing parks deserved to be expanded. The Club's champion in this effort would be a congressman from San Francisco, Phillip Burton. Congressman Burton huddled with Ed Wayburn and representatives from the White House and the National Park Service and drew up a long list of projects to round out the national park system. It included nine new or enlarged national parks, fourteen new wilderness areas, eight new wild and scenic rivers, and three new national trails. It added Mineral King to Sequoia National Park. Phil Burton, one of the shrewdest political maneuverers ever to occupy a seat in the House, managed to build overwhelming support for the bill in Congress by including some tidbit in nearly every congressional district. A new urban parks program was born. The Santa Monica Mountains National Recreation Area was established near Los Angeles. Nine new historic parks were created.

Burton's enemies, opponents of expansion of the federal parks system, saw the steamroller coming and tried to derail it by calling it a "parkbarrel," but they never stood a chance. The conservationists had done their work well, and the public was in firm support of park-system expansion. The Omnibus Parks Bill passed by overwhelming voice vote in October 1978, the largest one-stroke expansion of the park system ever accomplished to that point. It had occupied Sierra Club members and staff and others throughout the country for months and years. Finally, it was law.

❧

AT HOME...AND ABROAD

By the late 1970s the Sierra Club had grown to around 175,000 members. There were by this time forty-five chapters with many groups within them. As a way to provide structures through which members could make their views known, several new institutions had been created. First, in the mid-fifties, was the Sierra Club Council, composed of one representative from each chapter. The council met at the same time as the board, and offered advice on conservation policy and institutional matters. And the Sierra Club's reach steadily spread. Membership began to build strongly outside California, and new chapters were formed in the Rockies, New England, and Florida. The Great Lakes Chapter, which had encompassed much of the Midwest, split into eight separate chapters, with strong memberships and vigorous leaders, several of whom went on to win election to the national board of directors. In 1972 the Canadian group of the Pacific Northwest Chapter coalesced to become the Western Canada Chapter, and a year later the Ontario Group of the Atlantic Chapter became the Ontario (now Eastern Canada) Chapter.

At the same time, the need for regional cooperation began to be felt, and Regional Conservation Committees were formed in California and the Midwest, composed of delegates from their constituent chapters. The chairs of these RCCs became regional vice-presidents of the Club.

Then, later in the seventies, a series of issue committees came into being, to discuss conservation matters that concern the Club as a whole, including energy and the environmental effects of nuclear war. By the eighties, the meetings of board, council, regional vice presidents, and issue committees were so large and complicated that they came to be called the "Circus."

Also by the seventies, outings were visiting nearly every state and a number of foreign countries. Concern for the environment outside the United States, which had been controversial during Brower's tenure, became widespread, partly as a result of the Club's foreign outings and the opportunities that members had to encounter foreign landscapes and indigenous peoples at first hand.

In 1972 the Club sent representatives to the United Nations' first Conference on the Human Environment in Stockholm, where governmental and nongovernmental representatives mingled for two weeks, became acquainted, and tried to divine ways of working together to their mutual benefit. Out of that grew a volunteer International Committee and an international office in New York, where Club volunteers and staff provided information and persuasion to the United Nations and its affiliated agencies. From that, in turn, grew the first internationally focused wilderness conference, known as "Earthcare," held in New York City in 1975.

Among the topics discussed at the Earthcare Conference was the thorny one of the population explosion. Population had been discussed at prior Wilderness Conferences, but little was done besides talking. In 1968, however, Ballantine Books and the Sierra Club had copublished a paperback titled *The Population Bomb* by Paul Ehrlich of Stanford, a book that Brower had encouraged him to write. Ehrlich argued in stark and forceful terms that all humanity and the very planet it depends on are headed for disaster if the growth of human numbers is not brought under control and, eventually, reversed. He observed that all causes are lost causes without population control. The book—which sold more than two million copies—helped stir the public's interest in what up to then had been of concern mainly to mathematicians and demographers; population would thenceforth be very much on the Sierra Club's mind. It was another example of the expansion of the Club's concerns.

ALASKA: SAFEGUARDING THE GREAT LAND

The Club had already fought several skirmishes over Alaska—Admiralty Island and the pipeline being foremost among them—and had begun building a case for the preservation of large tracts as wilderness, as national parks, as wildlife refuges, and as wild rivers. It would be a complicated effort. Not only were there loggers and miners with fates other than wilderness in mind for Alaska, there were also native Alaskans, who had been pleading for years for title to a fair share of their ancestral homelands.

Nineteen seventy-one saw passage of the Alaska Native Claims Settlement Act, which set up a complicated system of land grants through village corporations and regional corporations. It allowed the natives and their governing bodies to select forty-four million acres of land to live on and develop. The law encouraged, even required, natives to go into business.

The Act also empowered the Secretary of the Interior, a Marylander named Rogers Morton, to withdraw from possible selection by the natives up to 80 million acres of land for consideration as national parks, national forests, wildlife refuges, or wild and scenic rivers. The Sierra Club came forward eagerly with a list of areas more than qualifying for preservation, and began to press its case in the Interior Department.

ABOVE TOP
Galen Rowell. The Summit of Mount Whitney, California. 1987. The population explosion is felt even on mountain peaks.

ABOVE
A cartoon reprinted in *Sierra.* © 1983 Jimmy Margulies, reprinted by permission *Houston Post*

William Garnett. Urban sprawl, San Francisco. 1967. Sierra Club Archives

Art Wolfe. Denali (Mount McKinley), Denali National Park, Alaska. 1987. Alaska—the name comes from a Native word meaning "the Great Land"—is America's biggest, wildest, least populated state. Its throngs of species evoke the days before Europeans arrived, when most of the North American continent was a paradise for wildlife. Perhaps the greatest feature of the Great Land is Mount McKinley, 20,320 feet high, named for a president who never saw his namesake. The Natives called the mountain "Denali"— "the Great One"—and the Sierra Club has fought many battles on behalf of it and its surrounding national park. Club staff and volunteers continue working to keep its one road free of cars, to expand its boundaries, to protect its wildlife, and to control mining in its streams.

Art Wolfe. Dall Ram above the Teklanika
River, Denali National Park, Alaska.
1988

David C. Fritts. Brown Bear, Alaska.
1982

Art Wolfe. Walrus, Round Island, Bering Sea, Alaska. 1987. Weighing about a ton and a half each, some fifteen thousand Pacific walrus bulls gather here every summer.

Art Wolfe. Snowy Owlets, Arctic Coastal Plain, Arctic National Wildlife Refuge, Alaska. 1988

M. *Woodbridge Williams.* Upper Nabesna Glacier and Mount Blackburn, in the Wrangell–St. Elias region of southeast Alaska. n.d. National Park Service

Charlie Ott. Barren-ground caribou in migration on a glacial river bar, interior Alaska. The annual caribou migration was a major concern of opponents of the Trans-Alaska pipeline as it is of those today opposed to opening the Arctic National Wildlife Refuge to oil drilling. n.d. Sierra Club Archives

The Club's interest in Alaska went all the way back to its founder. Muir was utterly fascinated by the Great Land, as the natives call it without exaggeration, and he was particularly enthralled with the glaciers, as he had been by the Sierra's tiny remnants. He wrote of one in Alaska:

> In the evening, after witnessing the unveiling of the majestic peaks and glaciers and their baptism in the down-pouring sunbeams, it

seemed inconceivable that nature could have anything finer to show us. Nevertheless, compared with what was to come the next morning, all that was as nothing. The calm dawn gave no promise of anything uncommon. Its most impressive features were the frosty clearness of the sky and a deep, brooding stillness made all the more striking by the newborn bergs. . . .

When the highest peak began to burn, it did not seem to be steeped in sunshine, however glorious, but rather as if it had been thrust into the body of the sun itself. . . .[26]

The sheer size and variety of the Alaskan wilderness were then understood and appreciated by very few people outside the state. From the rain forest and the fjords in the southeast to Denali, the continent's tallest mountain, in the central part of the state, from the massive herds of caribou in the north, to rivers everywhere teeming with char, grayling, and salmon, Alaska was the biggest piece of nearly pure wilderness left on the planet outside Antarctica. It was also the site of rich mineral deposits, some in awkward places, like the petroleum beneath the North Slope and the gold in Denali's streams, which would inevitably lead to bitter conflict.

The Club's major involvement with Alaska began with the Wayburns' visit in 1967, and it grew steadily more intense through their efforts and those of many others. With the arrival of the Carter administration in Washington, a determined cadre of Alaskans, supported by Sierra Club staff in San Francisco and Washington, D.C., and other members throughout the country, reminded the public that Alaska is ninety-nine percent federal land—it belongs to all the people of the United States, at least most of it does. Therefore the interests of all the people are equal, they concluded, and economic development for private gain should not necessarily take precedence over preservation of wildlife, natural resources, and scenic beauty.

Secretary Morton had taken an important step by giving temporary protection to 83.4 million acres of land in Alaska in 1973. That protection ran out five years later. Those six years saw national environmental organizations pour great effort into building public support for Alaskan preservation efforts. Indeed, on the eve of the expiration of the Morton withdrawal, the House of Representatives voted approval—by nine to one—for a remarkably strong bill that permanently protected much of Alaska's most important wild areas. But using the unique rules of the Senate, Alaska's two senators were able to kill the bill through filibuster.

At this point, President Carter and his interior secretary, Cecil Andrus, rode to the rescue, and used their considerable powers under the Antiquities Act and other statutes to set aside approximately 56 million acres of national monuments and another 40 million acres of national wildlife refuges in the forty-ninth state.

Carter had done what he could. The conservationist organizations took the initiative. Operating as the Alaska Coalition, chaired by the Club's Chuck Clusen, they mounted what has been universally acclaimed as the best coordinated, best staffed, most sophisticated environmental lobbying assault that

Frank LaRoche. Muir Glacier, from Glacier Bay. 1893. From Dave Bohn, *Glacier Bay: The Land and the Silence* (San Francisco: Sierra Club, 1967).

J. F. Morse. Muir cabin, Alaska, Muir standing at left. 1890. From Dave Bohn, *Glacier Bay.*

John Muir spent eleven days alone on the glacier that bears his name in Alaska, dragging his hundred-pound sled across crevasses and ice bridges, making sketches and filling his journals with scientific observations. He made five trips to Alaska in all, between 1879 and 1899. He was working on the manuscript for *Travels in Alaska* when he died in 1914.

Lomen Bros. In 1881, John Muir joined a rescue expedition in Alaska aboard this ship, the S. S. *Corwin,* in search of the lost steamer *Jeannette* and her crew. Muir described the journey in his book *The Cruise of the Corwin.* Photograph dated 1910. Sierra Club Archives

Anon. In 1880, John Muir and other naturalists accompanied an expedition to Alaska sponsored by E. H. Harriman, later president of the Southern Pacific Railroad. Here the party observes ice cliffs, stranded icebergs, and part of the front wall of a glacier. Sierra Club Archives

Art Wolfe. Icy Bay, Alaska. 1988

Washington had ever seen. The Coalition represented virtually every environmental organization in the country, large and small. It had volunteer organizers — most of them Club activists — in nearly every congressional district, and several in the key ones whose congressman sat on the critical committees. It persuaded stores that sell camping equipment to distribute save-Alaska literature to their customers. It ran newspaper advertisements, stimulated magazine articles, recruited celebrities.

As the decade closed, and the Carter administration prepared to give way to Ronald Reagan, Congress passed the Alaska National Interest Lands Conservation Act, by far the biggest single land preservation law ever enacted. Carter signed it on December 2, 1980. ANILCA, at a stroke, doubled the size of the national park system, trebled the size of the national wildlife refuge system, and trebled the amount of territory set aside as wilderness. Altogether, the law protected 104 million acres, an extraordinary amount of spectacular land.

But the 1980s would see a dramatic turn in the relationship between conservationists in private organizations and government officials. Although the Carter administration had been at odds with conservationists over several matters — support for building nuclear power plants and the creation of the Energy Mobilization Board, to name two of the most important — the relationship had been more cordial than it had been since the thirties. How the Reagan administration would treat environmental affairs was unknown, but there were ominous portents. Environmentalists who had served in the Carter administration quickly began to look for posts back in the private nonprofit world. The Sierra Club drew a nervous breath and waited to see what the Californian's presidency would mean.

National Park System

Non-Wilderness

Wilderness

1. Aniakchak NM & P
2. Bering Land Bridge NPr
3. Cape Krusenstern NM
4. Denali NP & Pr
5. Gates of the Arctic NP & Pr
6. Glacier Bay NP & Pr
7. Katmai NP & Pr
8. Kenai Fjords NP
9. Kobuk Valley NP
10. Lake Clark NP & Pr
11. Noatak NPr
12. Wrangell-St. Elias NP & Pr
13. Yukon-Charley Rivers NPr

Abbreviations: N = National, P = Park,
Pr = Preserve, M = Monument

Bureau of Land Management System
Conservation Areas

14. Steese National Conservation Areas
15. White Mountain National
    Recreation Area

National Wild and Scenic Rivers System
Rivers

National Forest System

Non-wilderness

Wilderness added in 1980

Wilderness added in 1990

16. Chugach National Forest
17. Tongass National Forest
18. Admiralty Island National Monument
19. Misty Fjords National Monument

National Wildlife Refuge System

Non-Wilderness

Wilderness

20. Alaska Maritime NWR*
21. Alaska Peninsula NWR
22. Arctic NWR
23. Becharof NWR
24. Innoko NWR
25. Izembek NWR
26. Kanuti NWR
27. Kenai NWR
28. Kodiak NWR
29. Koyukuk NWR
30. Nowitna NWR
31. Selawik NWR
32. Tetlin NWR
33. Togiak NWR
34. Yukon Delta NWR
35. Yukon Flats NWR

*The Alaska Maritime National Wildlife
Refuge consists of all the public lands in
the coastal waters and adjacent seas of
Alaska, including islands, islets, rocks,
reefs, capes, and spires.

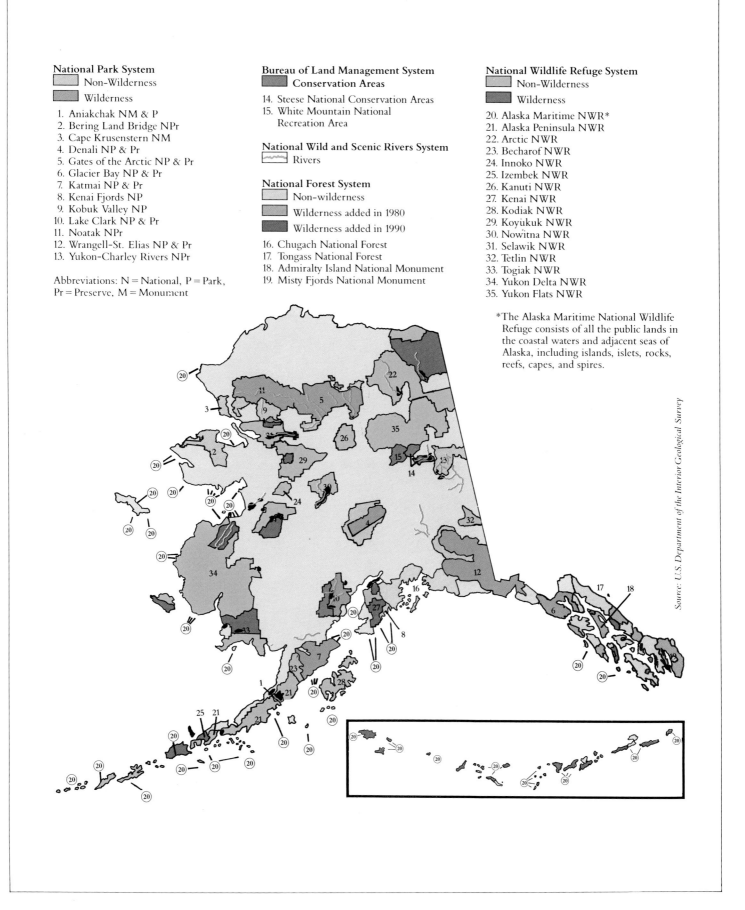

Source: U.S. Department of the Interior Geological Survey

STRETCHING THE BOUNDARIES

❧

THE SIERRA CLUB, THE ENVIRONMENTAL MOVEMENT, AND THE WORLD
1980 ❧ 1990

The 1980s would see the emergence of yet another Sierra Club, a larger version of its traditional self, but one that was different as well, as the old California roots became less important, the geographic diversity of the membership continued to increase, and the sheer size and scope of the organization mushroomed.

Much of the credit for the surge of membership in the Sierra Club in the 1980s goes to the presidential administration of Ronald Reagan, whose personnel and policies had a similar effect on the entire environmental movement. For the Sierra Club, membership more than tripled in ten years, soaring from 182,000 in 1980 to 600,000 by mid-1990.

Tentatively in the seventies, more boldly in the eighties, environmental organizations, with the Sierra Club at the forefront, dipped their toes in the treacherous waters of electoral politics (finding it easier to be persuasive with someone they had helped to elect). The decade also witnessed the emergence of environmental groups dedicated to direct confrontation with authority and to civil disobedience, groups that disdained working within the political system almost entirely. The two most prominent were Greenpeace and Earth First! Greenpeace, born in western Canada, had nautical beginnings, first sailing to Amchitka Island in the Aleutians and Mururoa in French Polynesia to protest nuclear bomb tests, later confronting whalers at sea to interfere with their hunts. Earth First! was created by disillusioned staff members from The Wilderness Society who felt that the Society, the Sierra Club, and other established groups were straying from their principles and tending to compromise with prodevelopment forces too readily.

These new groups, in part, would lead the Sierra Club and others to reexamine the composition of their organizations, their activities, and their public images as the decade drew to a close.

By the end of the decade, as the Club approached its centennial, it was universally acknowledged that the environment was at or near the top of every list of issues that concerned people and governments around the world.

The opening-up of Eastern Europe revealed industrial pollution of almost unimaginable proportions, while at the same time demonstrating that environmental activists in places like Romania and Czechoslovakia could be instrumental in bringing profound changes to their political systems, helping to force out the old regimes and bringing in new ones determined to clean up factories and reverse the ubiquitous contamination of air, water, soil, and food supplies. What started with bird watchers in the Audubon Society and mountain climbers in the Sierra Club had become a major concern of people throughout the world. The Club's statement of purpose, revised in 1981, now reads, "to explore, enjoy, and protect the wild places of the earth, to practice and promote the responsible use of the earth's ecosystems and resources; to educate and enlist humanity to protect and restore the quality of the natural and human environment; and to use all lawful means to carry out these objectives." Innumerable citizens of planet earth have come to share the Sierra Club credo.

"TO EXPLORE, ENJOY, AND PROTECT..."

By 1980, the Sierra Club and its members were not only embroiled in saving land from destructive development, chemical contamination, and other assaults, but were also enjoying it in large numbers and in a growing number of places, both domestic and foreign.

Until the 1950s the driving forces of the outings program had been mountaineering and rock climbing in the United States. As the Club grew in raw numbers, the climbers became less central to the organization's inner workings. So they banded together, designing excursions to the most challenging cliffs and spires around the world, including the sheer faces of the old homeland, Yosemite. By the late fifties, Club climbers had finally pinned their way up the vertical walls of El Capitan and Half Dome, and had begun their own journal, *Ascent*, to publish the celebrations and accounts that the *Bulletin* no longer had room for. They organized expeditions to high peaks abroad as well—to Canada, South America, and Asia, including the first ascent of the West Ridge of Mount Everest in the early 1960s.

There were plenty of members who were not hardy enough to climb Everest, of course, and remained happy to go along on Club outings simply for the flowers, or the fishing, or the simple beauty and exhilaration of the outdoors. As membership burgeoned in the 1950s (from five thousand to sixteen thousand during the decade), members were attracted to activities other than conquering mountains.

One activity that became very popular beginning at this time was river-running. The first Club-sponsored river trip had been put together in 1953 to stimulate interest in the campaign to block dams in Dinosaur National Monument, and it was a great success, both as a tactic (the dams were blocked) and as plain good fun. The Club decided to continue the practice, and the Outing Committee—a volunteer group of trip leaders who oversaw the outings program—decided to establish a permanent river-running sub-committee.

California rivers were used as training sites for boatmen, but they were not long enough for a one- or two-week outing. For that, the Club generally went to the Colorado Plateau, later to the north and northwest, to challenge the Snake, the Salmon, and the Rogue rivers. In the middle 1950s the Sierra Club was the biggest sponsor of river trips in the country and probably therefore in the world. Mountain trips were booming as well.

This was the heyday of the Sierra Club outing, at least measured in numbers. In the late fifties, approximately five thousand Sierra Club members (or one in three) were participating in Sierra Club outings—national outings, that is, as opposed to trips sponsored by chapters, which were and are a prominent part of local activities.

By the 1970s there were dozens of Sierra Club trips, exploring Alaska, the Southwest, the Rockies, and Appalachians, and many other places, with gear carried on foot, mule, burro, horse, skis, bicycles, boats, rafts—and even on wheels: some trips in Hawaii and the Southwest moved people and equipment from campsite to campsite in automobiles.

All these outings combined historical and cultural interests with hiking and mountaineering, and they made a point of making contact with local environmental and mountaineering organizations as far as possible. Just as the Club was a pioneer of wilderness river-rafting trips, it is no exaggeration to say that these outings helped spawn the now-enormous adventure travel industry. The early organizers of the Club's overseas trips later created a commercial travel business called Mountain Travel, which proved that organizing and conducting such trips could be profitable. Mountain Travel now has a hundred imitators, and the people who have discovered foreign wilderness for themselves have swelled the ranks of conservation activists further.

ABOVE TOP
Martin Litton. Native flora and fauna are obliterated by dune buggies and other vehicles on Nipomo Dunes, near Pismo Beach, California. c. 1963. Sierra Club Archives

ABOVE
Anon. Motorcycle races across the Mojave Desert have long been opposed by the Sierra Club because of their damage to the fragile desert ecosystem. Dirt-bike enthusiasts have recently formed an organization called the Sahara Club in deliberate parody (as well as serious opposition). n.d. Sierra Club Archives

OPPOSITE RIGHT
B. Nation / Sygma. A cleanup effort after the *Exxon Valdez* oil spill. 1989. In March 1989 the Exxon Corporation tanker went aground in Prince William Sound, releasing eleven million gallons of Alaskan crude oil. Over 700 miles of beach were soaked and thousands of birds and marine animals died. It was America's worst oil spill and the costliest settlement for damages to date.

Galen Rowell. Porters at Concordia, Karakoram Himalaya, Pakistan. 1975

Galen Rowell. Celebrating the Return to Green Grass at Urdukas, Karakoram Himalaya, Pakistan. 1975. These mountaineers are returning from an ascent of K2, the world's second highest peak, on an expedition funded in part by a book advance from the Sierra Club.

OPPOSITE
Galen Rowell. First Descent, Braldu River, Karakoram Himalaya, Pakistan. 1984. Today the frontiers of adventure are in Alaska, Antarctica, the highest reaches of the Andes, and here the Himalaya of Pakistan.

224

Galen Rowell. Moonlight at Concordia, Karakoram Himalaya, Pakistan. 1987

Not all Sierra Club trips were solely for pleasure and recreation. Service trips — subsidized by fees from other outings and organized in cooperation with the Park Service, the Forest Service, or other agencies — take people into the wilds to clean up trash, build new trails, restore trails, reroute existing trails around degraded meadows, even remove the wreckage from crashed airplanes (strange to say, a particularly popular activity). Service trips, begun in 1958, have become more numerous as the popularity of backpacking has burgeoned — therefore increasing wear and tear on the wilderness.

In 1971 members in the San Francisco Bay Chapter began Inner City Outings, a program that takes inner-city children, along with disabled people of all ages, into the out-of-doors for hikes and campouts. This is a chapter-run volunteer activity, underwritten by grants from various sources, and is considered of prime importance as the Sierra Club continues its effort to broaden its membership base. As of 1990, the ICO program was running as many as three hundred trips a year, with up to three thousand participants, organized by thirty different Sierra Club chapters.

In 1985 the outings program ran up against a difficult problem that has plagued institutions across the country providing recreation services: the soaring cost of liability insurance. The crisis was slow in coming to the Club, but by 1985 only one insurance company would offer this insurance and the price was exorbitant. In 1988 the board of directors was forced to cancel all climbing activities — national and local — requiring ropes, ice axes, and so forth, and to curtail river trips, owing to unaffordable insurance premiums. This move precipitated an attempted palace revolution in the Club, when a group of climbers from Southern California mounted unsuccessful campaigns for seats on the board of directors in 1989 on a platform based on spending more money on insurance in order to revive Sierra Club-sponsored technical rock climbing. Once upon a time a crisis in rock climbing might well have become a burning issue within the Club as a whole; by 1989 it was overshadowed by other concerns.

THE IMPORTANCE OF BEING POLITICAL

Persuasion of legislators has engaged Sierra Club members since the Club's founding. Over the years it became obvious that if Club members could help to select legislators, they would have an easier time winning battles in Congress. When an unincorporated League of Conservation Voters was founded in 1969 to rate candidates and make endorsements in key races, the Club's executive director joined other national leaders on its steering committee. But until 1974, neither the Sierra Club nor any other incorporated organization could participate directly in elective politics. That year Congress passed a law reforming the way campaigns for the Senate and the House of Representatives are run and financed. It was perhaps the decade's single most important development for the Sierra Club and the environmental movement in general.

The key provision of the new law had gone unnoticed until Carl Pope, the associate conservation director of the Club, browsed through the new statute and realized that the Sierra Club and other groups could, if they chose to, participate at the beginning of the process of creating law. The board of directors embarked on a long debate about whether the Sierra Club ought to take the plunge into electoral politics.

The first step was cautious. In 1976, the board created the Sierra Club Committee on Political Education, which helped favored candidates by publicizing their environmental records but stopped short of endorsing them. Several California chapters experimented with this new activity, while most members outside California waited to see how the experiment would work. Some Club volunteer leaders put together committees of "Conservationists for Candidate X" and used chapter mailing lists to promote X's campaign.

Some months before the congressional elections of 1980, Mike McCloskey was on a lobbying visit to Washington, D.C., and met with Senator John Culver of Iowa, a strong environmentalist. Culver remarked that the environmentalists in Congress were in trouble, that their programs were therefore in trouble, and that they needed help.

McCloskey took the message to the board. Again the board proceeded carefully. In that first year, 1980, the Club raised and dispensed about $100,000 to support candidates in several key races, but did not actually endorse any national candidate by name. As an experiment, the Club endorsed several candidates for election to the California legislature in Sacramento, most of whom won. The national experiment was less successful, mainly because the Reagan tide washed away many strong environmentalists, particularly in the Senate, despite the Club's help.

The Club thereupon decided that half measures were insufficient. In 1982 it endorsed about 140 candidates for the House and the Senate and raised around a quarter of a million dollars for their campaigns. More than that, members themselves worked on campaigns. Around three quarters of the Club-endorsed candidates won. In 1984, the Club endorsed Walter Mondale's challenge to Ronald Reagan. For what it was worth, the participation of the Club and other environmental organizations in the Mondale campaign helped persuade the Democratic Party to adopt a strong environmental platform. (The election was still a landslide for Ronald Reagan.)

Results in the Congress were much better. As in 1982, something like three-quarters of the Club-endorsed candidates prevailed. All campaigns are complicated, of course, and the environmental issues are only rarely the decisive ones. Nevertheless, conservationist support helped win a number of extremely important races and helped maintain the congressional breakwater of forces trying to resist the Reagan anti-environment battleship.

Political activity nationally remained fairly constant throughout the eighties, with the Club endorsing nearly two hundred candidates for the House and Senate. It endorsed neither George Bush nor Michael Dukakis in the 1988 election, though many members worked for the governor's campaign, a few for the vice president's. It is hard to get a firm count of state and local election activity by Club members, committees, groups, and chapters, but

Roxanne Kjarum. A Club member wields a pickaxe to help build a new trail, on a service trip to the Marble Mountain Wilderness in northern California. c. 1980. Sierra Club Archives

such activity grew dramatically during the decade, particularly as politicians came to value the endorsement of environmentalists more and more. During the 1992 election cycle, the Club's political committee planned to raise and spend a million dollars.

❧

THE SECRETARY FROM WYOMING

If ever there was a watershed in the history of the American conservation movement, it came on the fourth of November in 1980, when Jimmy Carter was swept from the White House and Ronald Reagan was swept in. In his latter days as governor of California—and particularly during the time he was a retired governor and presidential candidate (from 1974 to 1980)—Reagan had become a darling of the far right for his social views. In his environmental policies as governor he had been moderate—even indifferent. As in his later years, his personal interest in the environment ran heavily to riding horses and chopping brush. Fortunately for conservationists, Governor Reagan's Secretary of Resources, approximately analogous to the federal Secretary of the Interior, had been Norman B. "Ike" Livermore, a packer, lumberman, wilderness advocate, originator of the Club's wilderness conferences, and a Sierra Club director from 1941 to 1949. During his tenure as Secretary of Resources, Ike Livermore helped to persuade Governor Reagan to oppose a trans-Sierra highway through Mammoth Pass, just to the south of Yosemite, and the giant Dos Rios reservoir on the Eel River. During his gubernatorial administration, Reagan had also acceded, though not with much enthusiasm, to the creation of a Redwood National Park on the Northern California coast.

But almost as soon as the presidential-election ballots were counted, disquieting rumors began to circulate through environmental organizations. Reagan, it was said, had telephoned Joseph Coors, the brewer, to ask for advice on choosing an interior secretary. Coors's first choice was thought to be Clifford Hansen, former senator from Wyoming, but Hansen reportedly declined the job, fearing that his family's lucrative public-land grazing permits might be jeopardized. In December the announcement was made. Reagan would appoint as his Secretary of the Interior a Wyoming-bred, Washington-trained lawyer named James Gaius Watt, then serving as president of the Mountain States Legal Foundation in Denver. Journalists scurried to their clipping files to find out what they could about Mr. Watt.

What they found was the sketchy history of a man oddly equipped for the top conservation job in the world. Watt had served in the middle reaches of the Interior Department during the Nixon administration, then on the Federal Power Commission in the mid-1970s. His Mountain States Legal Foundation was a prodevelopment counterpart to the Sierra Club Legal Defense Fund. It was nonprofit, but it was supported by and usually represented the interests of mining companies, loggers, dam builders, stockmen, and real estate developers in the Rocky Mountains.

230

Another facet of the Watt personality was his fundamentalism. During one congressional committee hearing, for example, Watt suggested that long-term stewardship of resources was not the ultimate concern since Armageddon might be just around the corner. His remark was blown somewhat out of proportion by alarmed conservationists and sensation-seeking reporters, but Watt's words and actions relating to the environment could hardly have been more antithetical to what most people took conservation to mean. He spoke of the nation's conservation organizations, the Sierra Club most decidedly included, as made up of "environmental extremists"; he decried the locking up of resources in wilderness areas and parks; he said there were two kinds of people in the country: "liberals and Americans." He found the Grand Canyon "tedious" after two days of a four-day trip. He liked wheels and he liked horses. As to other forms of transportation, he chuckled, "I don't like to paddle and I don't like to walk." He undoubtedly would have agreed with the assessment of Edwin Meese, first a White House advisor and later Attorney General, who tried to paint conservationists with the brush of elitism: "My definition of a Sierra Club member is someone who *already* has a house at Lake Tahoe."

James Watt's first major policy statement came in a speech he delivered to a convention of national park concessionaires, people who run the closely regulated private businesses in national parks and monuments, the monopolies allowed into the parks since the turn of the century to provide needed services to the public. Watt said he was sympathetic to their concerns, and that previous administrations had not allowed enough development in the parks. He said he would not pursue the creation of any new parks or the enlargement of any existing ones, as conservation groups were urging. He claimed that what was needed was the rebuilding of roads and hotels and other facilities in the parks and the construction of new ones. He suggested turning more functions over to concessionaires. He even recommended handing total management of the Golden Gate and Gateway National Recreation Areas to state or local governments.

Then he got down to business. While the Wilderness Act allowed mining claims in wilderness areas until 1984, the Interior Department — which manages mineral leasing both on its own lands and on those of the Forest Service — had actually approved very few applications to explore for minerals such as oil in wilderness areas. Watt decided to change all that. He ordered the issuance of mineral-exploration permits in one of the oldest and largest wilderness areas then in existence, a sort of icon to the wilderness movement, the Bob Marshall Wilderness in Montana. Named for the cofounder of The Wilderness Society, this area comprises roughly a million and a half acres on the west slope of the Continental Divide, and its high mountain peaks, forests, and valleys are home to grizzlies, elk, and many other wild creatures. "The Bob" was said to be one of just two places in the contiguous forty-eight states where it was possible to get ten miles away from a road. (The other was in Sequoia National Park in California; its nearest road-head was in Mineral King Valley.)

W. A. Jackson. Removing debris from the east fork of the Toklat River, Denali Wilderness, Alaska, on a 1981 service trip. Sierra Club Archives

Rick Bradley. On a service trip to the Trinity Alps, northern California. 1969. Sierra Club Archives

Carr Clifton. Fireweed, Bob Marshall
Wilderness, Montana. 1989

Carr Clifton. The Chinese Wall, Bob
Marshall Wilderness, Montana. 1989

232

Galen Rowell. Three Climbers on Mount Everest's West Ridge at 24,000 Feet, Tibet. 1983

Watt apparently cared nothing about disturbing that pristine remoteness. His philosophy in this regard was that resources, all resources, should be developed now, in a deliberate and orderly fashion, so as to avoid sloppy, helter-skelter development when they really came into short supply in the future. The secretary evidently put no stock in the argument that some places should be altogether off-limits to development.

Faced with his proposal for the Bob Marshall Wilderness, the national conservation community rose up as one, with much of the public in full and vocal support. Lobbyists for the organizations worked with the House Interior Committee, and the committee issued an order to Watt that he immediately withdraw the Bob and two adjoining wilderness areas in Montana — the Great Bear and the Scapegoat — from leasing. Watt grudgingly obeyed the order, while at the same time suggesting that it might be unconstitutional for a single congressional committee to issue such an order. In doing so he explicitly invited someone to file suit.

His old law firm, Mountain States Legal Foundation, was happy to oblige. The Sierra Club, through the Sierra Club Legal Defense Fund, intervened in the case, since it was clear that Watt wanted to lose it and would not defend his action as Interior Secretary well — if at all. Mountain States won that case when the Supreme Court — ruling in an unrelated case — threw out the idea of a one-house veto of an agency decision. The public outcry against wilderness leasing was so vociferous, however, even from Western members of Congress who would support Watt on most issues, that the House Interior Committee searched around and came up with another stratagem: it refused to let Watt spend any money on his leasing program. The wilderness areas were spared. Citizen conservationists throughout the country had prevailed.

Then Watt tried another tack. He announced that he had seen the light. He was putting all designated wilderness off-limits to mining and mineral exploration until the next century. Watt dropped this little bomblet during an appearance on *Meet the Press* one Sunday morning in response to a question from *The New York Times*'s Philip Shabecoff. Watt insisted that he had changed his views and would protect wilderness on behalf of all Americans alive and those yet to be born.

The press reported the story straight, with no analysis and little understanding of what Watt was actually proposing. Newspapers reported the conversion of the Interior Secretary. Conservationists were caught off guard and withheld immediate comment. When they had time to think about it, however, they realized the clumsy ploy Watt had tried. By the terms of the Wilderness Act, wilderness would be *permanently* off-limits to mineral-seeking entry as of the end of 1984 without any action by Congress, the Interior Department, or anyone else. What Watt had proposed, without putting it in so many words, was a drastic revision of the Wilderness Act to permit new entry into wilderness areas after the year 2000. When they realized what was afoot, conservationists and their congressional allies were outraged, and they said so. The idea died a quick, merciful death.

The Watt period in federal government was so bizarre, so outrageous, that it is easy to fix on the offbeat incidents and difficult to remember the serious damage that Watt and the rest of the Reagan administration did to the institutions of environmental protection. Many recall Watt's banishing of the Beach Boys from a Fourth of July celebration on the Mall in Washington because he disliked their image. Others recall reports of his taking time out from senior staff meetings, adjourning to a small room nearby, rolling on the floor, and speaking, it was said, in tongues. But more important, Watt and his colleagues did fundamental and lasting harm to the federal government's environmental agencies, reducing their budgets, shattering the morale of their staffs, and canceling popular and useful programs, like the Youth Conservation Corps, a sort of federal version of Sierra Club service outings. If Watt had been more adept at administration and public performance, the wrongs he did would have been more grave.

Watt also put the environmental establishment—the Sierra Club and all its kindred organizations—on the defensive. They shifted their efforts from creating parks and getting designation for wilderness areas and wild rivers to protecting existing ones and the agencies that manage them. Not surprisingly, Watt's and his colleagues' activities caused the greatest flowering of support for environmental organizations since Earth Day in 1970, a spurt in concern that saw the Club's membership shoot from 182,000 in 1980 to 440,000 in 1988 when Ronald Reagan stepped down. (A Sierra Club membership solicitation letter crossed Watt's desk one day, and he returned it to Mike McCloskey with the note, "I'm your best fundraiser." On the whole, he was right.)

In any event, after Watt had been in office only three months, the Sierra Club decided to go on the offensive. It announced a petition campaign to persuade Congress to oust the secretary. Friends of the Earth was cosponsor. Petitions were printed and distributed to all chapters and groups of both organizations, and they were received warmly and enthusiastically and carried to rallies and shopping centers and picnics. Watt had become the second most visible member of the administration after the president himself: no one was neutral on the subject of the secretary.

The petition campaign aimed to get a million signatures, and it received that and a hundred thousand more. The petitions were presented to the House Majority Leader, Tip O'Neill, and the Senate Minority Whip, Alan Cranston, by Club president Joe Fontaine and FOE president Rafe Pomerance on October 19, 1981. The ceremony took place on the steps of the Capitol, with Sierra Club volunteers from all fifty states present. Watt dismissed all 1.1 million signers as extremists and anti-Americans. People continued to join environmental organizations in unprecedented numbers.

The Watt years marked for the most part a stalemate in environmental matters. Watt tried to remake government in his image, and in that he mostly failed. The Sierra Club and its fellow organizations had to be content fending off the initiatives of the Interior Department and the Environmental Protection Agency and hoping for a better day. Watt lasted two more years, until October 9, 1983, when, as a member of the Cabinet, he put his foot into his

The cartoons reproduced in *Sierra* magazine summarized some of the concerns of conservationists during Ronald Reagan's first administration. Here is a sampling by Paul Conrad, Ed Stein, Dick Locher, and Jimmy Margulies. Right: © 1983 Paul Conrad, reprinted by permission *Los Angeles Times*. Below: Ed Stein, reprinted by permission *Rocky Mountain News*. Opposite above: Dick Locher, reprinted by permission Tribune Media Services. Opposite below: © 1986 Jimmy Margulies, reprinted by permission *Houston Post*.

"THE ENVIRONMENTAL EXTREMISTS WON'T BE SATISFIED UNTIL THE WHITE HOUSE LOOKS LIKE A BIRD'S NEST!"

OH, BEAUTIFUL! OUR FEDERAL LANDS
ON SALE FOR WAVES OF GREEN.
WANT A PURPLE MOUNTAIN MAJESTY?
THAT'LL BE A BUCK-NINETEEN!
AMERICA, AMERICA,
HERE'S WHAT THEY PLAN FOR THEE:
TO RAPE THY LAND FOR CASH IN HAND
FROM SEA TO SHINING SEA.

TREES
BY JAMES WATT

I THINK THAT I SHALL NEVER SEE
AN ENVIRONMENTALIST LOVELY AS A TREE

A TREE UNDER WHICH WE FIND
LAND WHICH SHORTLY WILL BE MINED

A TREE WHICH DOES NO ONE GOOD
UNLESS IT'S HARVESTED FOR WOOD

A TREE THAT WILL BY SUMMER BE
A REDWOOD DECK FOR YOU AND ME

A TREE THAT SOME YOUNG ECO-FREAK
FOR HIS CHILDREN WANTS TO KEEP

POLICY IS MADE BY FOOLS LIKE ME
NOT EVEN GOD CAN SAVE THIS TREE

mouth for the last time. Commenting on the diversity of a commission that had recently been appointed to advise the Interior Department, he characterized members as "a black, a woman, two Jews, and a cripple." The public outrage forced him to resign. This preempted a motion of no confidence then pending in the Senate, which would have been an informal but embarrassing rebuke, both for him and for President Reagan, who was about to plunge into a reelection campaign. Watt was replaced by William Clark, a long-time friend and associate of Reagan, who hunkered down and kept the Interior Department's name out of the newspapers until the 1984 election was safely over.

❧

POLLUTION POLITICS

Along with the signing of the National Environmental Policy Act, the most significant national environmental development of the year 1970 had been the creation of the Environmental Protection Agency via an executive order from President Nixon.

The Environmental Protection Agency was created largely to provide a federal presence to cope with pollution run wild in the United States. Those were the days when Lake Erie was declared "dead" from pollution, and when the Cuyahoga River caught fire in Cleveland because it was so heavily polluted with oil. Environmentalists, including people from the heavily polluted East who had begun to join organizations like the Sierra Club, began to demand that something drastic be done to clean up the rapidly deteriorating quality of air and water. The EPA began simply as an attempt to bring existing federal pollution control and related activities into one agency. By the 1980s the EPA was one of the biggest agencies of the federal government and seemed to be on the verge of becoming a department and its chief a full secretary in the cabinet.

In response to the public's concern and to scientific studies that corroborated what was easy to see in the oily waters and smudged skies, Congress passed a series of pollution laws and gave the EPA the job of carrying them out.

At first cooperation between the agency and groups like the Club was smooth. Sierra Clubbers found jobs in the agency, and when the Carter administration took power in 1976, several of the EPA's top positions were filled by self-described environmentalists. There is considerable debate over how well the EPA's regulatory approach to pollution control can ever work, considering the extent to which it relies on the monitoring and control of pollution rather than its elimination at the source, but, at least for the agency's first ten years, the people who ran it *tried* to make it work. That changed with the election of 1980.

That year Reagan appointed Anne Gorsuch, a Colorado legislator, as administrator of the EPA, and she immediately made it clear that she, like

James Watt at the Interior Department, was opposed to everything the Sierra Club and its colleague groups were for. It did not take a petition campaign to drive her from office. Scandal was so pungent around the EPA in the early 1980s—a chief deputy was actually sent to prison and Gorsuch herself became the highest executive branch official ever held in contempt of Congress—that she left office voluntarily in the spring of 1983, further limiting the administration's ability to do damage. Gorsuch was replaced by William D. Ruckleshaus, a widely respected administrator, who at age thirty-eight had been appointed to run the EPA when it was created.

THE SECOND
REAGAN ADMINISTRATION

Mush Emmons. Former Executive Director and current Club Chairman J. Michael McCloskey with stacks of "Replace Watt" petitions. 1981. Sierra Club Archives. If two thousand Oregon citizens had voted differently in 1962, Mike McCloskey would have been elected to the state legislature. Fortunately for the Club, he lost. McCloskey, a hiker and outdoorsman, began working for the Club and the Federation of Western Outdoor Clubs to prevent logging in his state's most spectacular wild valleys and, later, to protect them in a federal wilderness system. The Club's first field representative, he became its first conservation director, its second executive director, and its first chairman. In the last position, he concentrates on building international lines of communication and advising foreign environmentalists.

The Sierra Club and most of the other politically active organizations bravely endorsed Walter Mondale for election despite polls that made his cause look hopeless. The polls showed that the public by and large loved Mr. Reagan while they detested his environmental policies—another instance in which the president's personal charm and reassuring manner carried him and his administration on a popular wave over a very unpopular sea. Mondale said all the right things about the environment, but he lost badly in 1984.

As in the previous election, environmentalist-endorsed candidates for the House and the Senate did considerably better, once the president was subtracted from the equation.

The second Reagan administration was a little calmer than the first, given the absence of the belligerent Mr. Watt. Ruckleshaus repaired the Environmental Protection Agency to his satisfaction, if not to the satisfaction of all observers, and handed it over to Lee Thomas, a nonideological veteran of previous service in the agency.

Since Reagan had taken office, the EPA had floundered, with funds being choked off even as the work load increased. In 1986, Congress appeared poised to grant a big increase to the Superfund, a pot of money set aside to clean up abandoned waste pits, gas stations, and other areas severely contaminated with toxic chemicals whose owners could not be located. The administration opposed the plan, and much of the environmental community was busy on other pressing matters. Despite unpromising odds, the Club decided to take this problem on, to try to preserve adequate funding for the clean-up.

They initiated a newsletter, the *Superactivist*, and began to rally members to the campaign. All the field staff and 150 members from districts heavily affected by toxic wastes were brought to lobby in Washington. In the end a bill was passed providing $10 billion to the Superfund; the initial funding for the program had been $1.6 billion.

DONALD HODEL AND THE GHOST OF HETCH HETCHY

William Clark, meanwhile, took care of the Interior Department without distinguishing himself in any particular way, and in 1985 he bowed out to go back to California. The agency was turned over to Donald P. Hodel, who had presided over the Bonneville Power Administration when it was a major participant in a nuclear-power development scheme that resulted in the biggest bond default in American history. Hodel later served as Secretary of Energy under Reagan.

Hodel worried the Sierra Club and other organizations because he was smooth, polite, and shrewd—all the things Jim Watt wasn't. Hodel went quietly to work to advance the Watt agenda, to promote the development of public lands for their energy potential, to discourage the expansion of the national parks, and the like. Watt had so rejuvenated the environmental movement, though, that Hodel was not able to operate quite so surreptitiously as he would have liked, and much of his proposed damage was circumvented.

And then Hodel pulled a surprise that caught everyone off guard: he proposed the dismantling of O'Shaughnessy Dam, the draining of Hetch Hetchy Valley, and the returning of it to Yosemite National Park. The Sierra Club immediately endorsed the idea, as might be expected. Others were suspicious and withheld judgment, fearing a trick. Of course the political leaders of San Francisco howled about their water supply, though the valley's water was by that time of secondary importance, since San Francisco could get the same water downstream. In reality, the loss of Hetch Hetchy as a reservoir would mean a financial loss to San Francisco—in the neighborhood of $50 million a year, which the city earned (and still earns) by selling Hetch Hetchy electricity to customers in the San Joaquin Valley.

It seems to have been Hodel's own idea to dismantle O'Shaugnessy and drain Hetch Hetchy. So it was presented at the time and there is no evidence to contradict the story. Nor has evidence been supplied to corroborate the thesis that the idea was floated as a brilliant political trick to drive a wedge between the Sierra Club and the politicians from its hometown and thereby to consume a good deal of the Club's effort that might have been spent more productively on other campaigns. In any event, no matter what the motive, no matter what the source, the idea surged through the Club like a wave of electricity. The board of directors quickly endorsed the plan, pointing out that a dam-free Hetch Hetchy had been a Club objective for eighty years. *Sierra* published a long section on the matter. Club volunteers and staff gave speeches and wrote letters and took to the airwaves to support the scheme. Here was a chance to undo the grievous wrong perpetrated three generations before. What a wonderful way to celebrate the wisdom of John Muir!

Alas, all Hodel got out of his wonderful idea was agreement to conduct a study. John Herrington, Hodel's replacement as Secretary of Energy, publicly disagreed with the notion of demolishing the dam, and President Reagan's spokesmen carefully distanced themselves from the plan. It was an idea whose time had not quite yet come, but that will one day.

❧

BRANCHING OUT

As the public's interest in environmental protection grew, along with the membership rolls of the Sierra Club and other groups, the scope of the Club's interests inevitably broadened. Where once it was sufficient to oppose a timber sale simply to preserve a pristine watershed, it now became common to debate why the sale was proposed in the first place. Was growth the problem? Capitalism? Greed? This in turn brought tension to the ranks of the Sierra Club, when some members began to make very abstract arguments about very tangible matters.

In the late 1950s, for example, a group of members argued vehemently that the Sierra Club ought not to conduct outings at all, since overuse of wilderness would destroy it, and the Club should be the last to sponsor the ruination of wilderness. It was a purist position, which would lead some to break with the Club and similar organizations and seek clear, simple answers to the ever more complicated questions arising on all sides.

A group of former Wilderness Society staffers resigned from that organization's payroll and founded Earth First!, which some of them dubbed a "disorganization." They saw the Society and the Sierra Club as too willing to compromise with government and industry and promised "no compromise in defense of Mother Earth." They opposed *any* sacrifice of *any* wilderness for *any* purpose, and did not mind going to jail to make their point. They would perch in trees to try to stop their being cut down. They would lie in front of, even chain themselves to, bulldozers to stop road construction in roadless areas. This kind of action evoked two quite distinct reactions from Sierra Club directors, members, and staff. Some welcomed the self-proclaimed radicals on the theory that their presence would make the Club seem more reasonable, closer to the elusive middle of the road. The countervailing view was that the extremism of Earth First!ers would taint all environmentalists. A little of both has undoubtedly occurred. The ranks of Earth First! have grown steadily, though it remains minuscule compared to the Sierra Club or the other less radical organizations.

Another tangential force to emerge in the 1970s and 1980s calls itself "deep ecology," a scholarly and academic discipline that also disdains the mainstream organizations and calls for a radical simplification of lifestyles and a militant defense of wilderness and natural systems. Then there appeared the "bioregionalists," who believe that political boundaries should be redrawn with nature in mind, that local consumption of locally produced goods ought to be supported if not required.

Fred Lochner, Jr. Cooking breakfast on a 1974 knapsack outing in the Monarch Divide area of Kings Canyon National Park. Lightweight campstoves have replaced fires on all Sierra Club outings as downed wood grows scarce in the wilderness. Sierra Club Archives

OPPOSITE
Neil Hoos. The Sierra Club's "Wilderness," "Wildlife," "Engagement," and pocket calendars—all illustrated with remarkably detailed and painstakingly reproduced nature images in full color—are purchased by over a million Americans a year. 1991

All these schools of thought were registered by the Sierra Club and inspired debate among members and letters to the board and staff. As an institution, the Sierra Club clearly would not react to every new analysis of environmental danger and culpability, but one thing it could do was publish books and articles to give the new opinions a fair hearing.

Sierra Club Books had been prospering since 1975, and had branched out in many directions. As mentioned earlier, the publishing wing of the Club served three prime purposes: to publish meritorious books and other material that would be useful to the general public and help draw new people to the Club; to provide timely, useful, thought-provoking insights and information to Club members; and to earn a modest surplus to contribute to the general fund of the Club.

After a short stint with its headquarters in New York, the book publishing program returned to San Francisco in 1974 under the direction of Jon Beckmann, who had spent the previous ten years in the publishing business in New York and New England.

A calendar series, begun in 1968 to promote the Exhibit Format books, was expanded and became an extremely lucrative and much imitated institution. A series of "Battlebooks" had been tested, to provide ammunition for members and other activists on major issues of the day. A new series of "Totebooks" was instituted, guidebooks with rugged covers and rounded corners designed specifically to fit into a backpacker's knapsack or hip pocket.

The Exhibit Format series was continued, with titles on the Everglades, the slickrock country of the Southwest, Thoreau's New England, and the Pacific Coast. Many new formats were tried as well. An ambitious book on the wilderness of space called *Galaxies* was published in 1980, and despite its cover price of $75 it sold 100,000 copies. Photographic studies appeared, including some playful titles like *Dead Tech: A Guide to the Archaeology of Tomorrow.* A successful illustrated collection of the writings of Isak Dinesen was published to coincide with release of the movie version of *Out of Africa.*

All-text books have examined acid rain, genetic engineering, hazardous waste, the chemical accident at Bhopal, India, global warming, and many other current topics. Technical titles have appeared on appropriate technology, gardening, and other subjects, along with a vast and very successful series of adventure travel guides. The editors have also supported literature with environmental themes, publishing novels, a mystery, and two collections of poetry. A line of children's books, begun in 1977, has won award after award and continues to thrive.)

Critics may say that the Club disposed of new philosophies by publishing books about them, but the observation does indicate how the book program permits the organization to investigate many more subjects than there is room for on the Club's agenda for advocacy. In late 1990 the Club's annual production was about thirty adult books, six calendars, and fifteen books for

242

Sierra Club Wilderness Calendar 1991

WOLVES
Text and Photographic Selection by
CANDACE SAVAGE
Foreword by L. David Mech

A Sierra Club Special Edition Calendar 1991

Wilderness 1991
Sierra Club Engagement Calendar

THE HOME PLA

Sierra Club Wildlife Calendar

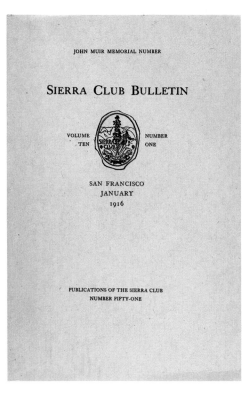

JOHN MUIR MEMORIAL NUMBER

SIERRA CLUB BULLETIN

VOLUME
TEN

NUMBER
ONE

SAN FRANCISCO
JANUARY
1916

PUBLICATIONS OF THE SIERRA CLUB
NUMBER FIFTY-ONE

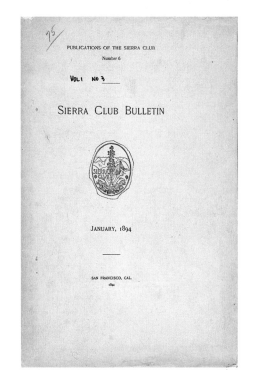

PUBLICATIONS OF THE SIERRA CLUB
Number 6

Vol I No 3

SIERRA CLUB BULLETIN

JANUARY, 1894

SAN FRANCISCO, CAL.
1894

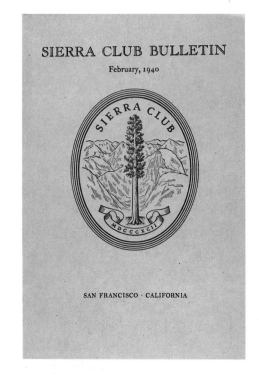

SIERRA CLUB BULLETIN

February, 1940

SAN FRANCISCO · CALIFORNIA

SIERRA CLUB BULLETIN

APRIL · 1941

PUBLISHED BY THE SIERRA CLUB · SAN FRANCISCO, CALIFORNIA

STARR KING CREEK   by Ansel Adams

SIERRA CLUB BULLETIN *June 1958*

SIERRA CLUB BULLETIN

November 1959

The pictures in my room are windows. . . .
They mean reality and beauty.
which arise like a song from the heart of the mountains.
—CEDRIC WRIGHT, 1889-1959

SIERRA CLUB BULLETIN

March-April 1964

Other people will want to be walking our trails,
up where the tree reaches high for the cloud,
up where the flower takes the summer wind with beauty,
and the summer rain too.
They will want to discover for themselves
the wildness that the ages have made perfect.
—DAVID BROWER
in "Wilderness Alps of Stehekin"

ELIOT PORTER: Galapagos

It is only a little planet . . .

Sierra Club Bulletin
Combined Annual Magazines 1966 1967 1968

1970 Wilderness Outings

Sierra Club Bulletin   ANNUAL OUTING ISSUE

A sampling of covers of the *Sierra Club Bulletin*. The Club's first publication has undergone fourteen face-lifts since the inaugural number appeared in 1893. Early on, it was published annually, and it presented articles about High Trips and climbing exploits, book reviews, and popular pieces on science and natural history. Reports on conservation issues appeared as well and have grown in importance with the Club. In 1981 the magazine became simply *Sierra*. One of the most prominent environmental journals, it has received eight "Maggies" since 1984, awarded by the Western Publications Association, and it was nominated for a 1989 National Magazine Award by the American Society of Magazine Editors for its special issue on American public lands. The covers reproducing photographs by Ansel Adams (1958), Cedric Wright (1959), and Eliot Porter (1966–68) suggest the Club's esthetic in photography, which has earned wide popular affection.

THE LAST REDWOODS

PHILIP HYDE and FRANCOIS LEYDET

Navajo Wildlands

"as long as the rivers shall run"

GLACIER BAY

The Land and the Silence

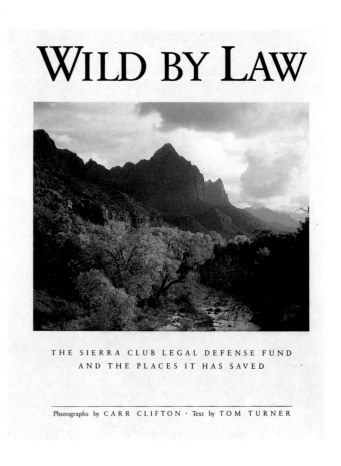

WILD BY LAW

THE SIERRA CLUB LEGAL DEFENSE FUND
AND THE PLACES IT HAS SAVED

Photographs by CARR CLIFTON · Text by TOM TURNER

WILDER SHORE

Morley Baer   David Rains Wallace

FOREWORD BY WALLACE STEGNER

From *Navajo Wildlands* (1967) by Philip
Hyde and Stephen C. Jett to *Alakshak*
(1989) by Art Wolfe and Art Davidson,
this selection of Sierra Club and Sierra
Club Legal Defense Fund books
suggests how its publishing program
continues to lobby for preservation by
showing — in eloquent photographs and
texts — what has been and what should
be preserved.

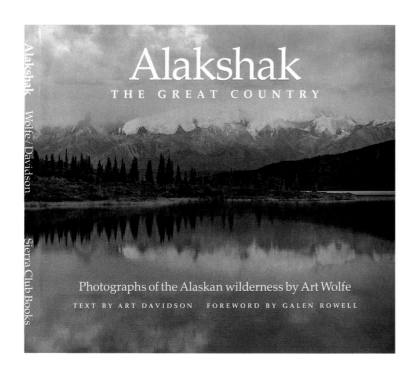

children and young readers. Other companies, under licensing agreements, produced Sierra Club note cards, jig-saw puzzles, posters, address books, and audio and video cassettes.

And, after a hiatus of sixteen years, the Club revived the full-page newspaper ad as a conservation tactic. Following the grounding of the oil tanker *Exxon Valdez* in Prince William Sound, Alaska, in March 1989, the Club took out an ad in *The New York Times* demanding that President Bush visit the site personally. (He didn't, but Club President Richard Cellarius did, and he reported the results of the spill disaster and the mismanaged cleanup in an article published in many chapter newsletters.) The ad solicited contributions to be used toward the clean up and to enable conservationists to monitor independently both the government and the oil company as restoration proceeded. Readers answered generously. The net proceeds, $120,000, were used, among other purposes, to subsidize volunteers' trips to the site of the spill to scrub beaches and rescue wildlife. Hundreds responded to the Club's plea for help, including the entire executive committee of the Hawaii Chapter's Kauai group, which spent five weeks on the scene in Seward.

In the summer of 1990, the Sierra Club warned, again via an advertisement in *The New York Times*, that the Iraqi invasion of Kuwait should not precipitate panic in the country's thinking about energy and should not lead to the oil companies' dictating energy policy. Rather, it called for passage of a bill then pending that would require more efficient automobiles, and it requested government action to stop oil and auto companies from exercising undue influence over public policy. The ad hit a sympathetic chord.

A SIERRA CLUB SNAPSHOT

It is August 23, 1990, in the Colby Library on the fourth floor of Club headquarters on Polk Street in San Francisco. The library suffered considerable damage during the World Series earthquake nearly a year ago, but all has been repaired. Some fifty people employed by Sierra Club chapters across the country have gathered to attend workshops and swap experiences and advice with their counterparts and members of the headquarters staff. Most appear to be between their mid-thirties and mid-forties, a handful older. Birkenstocks and sandals are outnumbered by running shoes and loafers, but not by much. Michael Fischer, executive director since 1987, is speaking.

"We have two big challenges ahead in the next ten years," he says. "The first is how to maintain the Club's unique structure as it gets larger. The second is how to enhance its ethnic diversity.

"People complain about the Club's bureaucracy, its inability to move quickly," he confesses. "But how can you run a six hundred and fifty thousand-member organization, soon to be a million, without a bureaucracy? How can you make quick decisions when there are so many people in positions of authority?" Greenpeace (now more than two million strong), he reports

Warren Marr. Mono Lake, California. 1989. Since 1980 the editors of *Sierra* magazine have held annual photography contests to showcase the talents of professionals and amateurs who focus on the natural landscape. This panorama by Warren Marr and the photograph by Mark Citret (see p. 261) were prizewinners for 1989. Rather than cash, the seventeen awards include cameras and outdoor equipment.

Jeff Gnass. January Morning, Zion National Park, Utah. 1979. Here and on the following pages are a selection of striking images reproduced in Sierra Club publications over the last decade or so.

John Ward. Independence Monument in Clouds, Colorado National Monument, New Mexico. 1988

Jeff Gnass. Winter Rabbitbrush and Hare Tracks, BLM Land on the Snake River Plain, Butte County, Idaho. 1987. "BLM" stands for the Bureau of Land Management, a federal agency.

Jeff Gnass. Hiker Overlooks Queens
Garden on the Navaho Loop Trail,
Bryce Canyon National Park, Utah.
1986

OPPOSITE
Willard Clay. Giant Red Paintbrush
Growing in a Lichen Bed, Kaibab
National Forest, Arizona. 1982

Philip Hyde. Grand Canyon National Park, Arizona, 1970

OPPOSITE
John Ward. Stormy Weather on the North Rim, from Indian Gardens, Grand Canyon National Park, Arizona. 1975

wistfully, has an appointed executive committee of four people that can decide anything for the organization. "This fierce democracy that is the Sierra Club is our greatest strength and our greatest challenge," he says diplomatically. "Other groups can move faster, but they can't touch the Sierra Club's highly evolved local structure."

Fischer quotes proudly from an article that has just been published in *Outside* magazine rating all the national environmental groups. It said, "in many locales, especially on the West Coast, the leading local environmental group is a Sierra Club chapter." One of Fischer's listeners asks, "Where does the Sierra Club fit into the spectrum of environmental groups?" A chapter staffer responds: "We're often described as the most radical of the mainstream groups. I like both halves of that, 'radical' and 'mainstream.' "

Fischer's second goal for the millennium, he says, is to broaden the ethnic diversity of Club membership, a challenge that has been recognized for at least two decades. A delegate from El Paso rises to urge rhetorically that the members of his executive committee abandon the suburbs and move with him into the inner city to experience at first hand how the people there live, how they suffer most from the effects of a degraded environment. Fischer announces creation of a new Club task force on ethnic diversity that will try to figure out new ways to attract people of color to the Club's fold. The discussion moves on to workshops on publicity, fundraising, and volunteer management.

Club members certainly have plenty to do. Poll after poll shows that the general public is willing to curtail the way it lives and to spend generously to safeguard environmental quality. Government, however, has still not got the message. Environmental activists across the land, frequently led by Sierra Club volunteers, are experimenting with ballot initiatives as a way to get laws enacted when the state legislature is slow, uninterested, or in thrall to the opposition. Public awareness is being heightened. Earth Day 1990 turned out millions of citizens worldwide to demonstrate their concern for the planet, and every Club chapter and many groups mounted activities of various sorts.

Movie stars and musicians are becoming aware of environmental issues and offering to help, lending their luster to initiative efforts and raising funds for political campaigns. The Club was a prime sponsor of ballot initiatives in California and elsewhere, to take the environmental case directly to the public. It seems evident that activities like this will continue and multiply.

The Sierra Club itself, as of 1990, is thriving. Membership growth shows no sign of abating. Members live about half in the West, half scattered throughout the rest of the country. They are well educated: seventy-eight percent have college degrees. They are politically active, voting twice as regularly and writing to public officials six times as often as the average citizen.

To avoid rising rents, the Club purchased an office building near the Civic Center in San Francisco in 1985, in close proximity to City Hall and state and federal office buildings. The national staff numbered 250, and were serving members from field offices in fifteen cities. There were fifty-seven chapters covering all states and Canada, sponsoring a wide variety of activities.

Mark Citret. Tree and Granite, Yosemite. 1977. This photograph won the first prize in the category of "Abstractions and Patterns" in *Sierra* magazine's photography contest for 1989. The other categories in the annual competition are "Landscape," "Wildlife," and "The Meeting of Land and Water" in both color and black and white.

Jeff Gnass. Spring Cottonwoods under a Stormy Sky, Grand Teton National Park, Wyoming. 1985

Philip Hyde. River Shore at Marble Gorge, Grand Canyon, Arizona. 1964

OPPOSITE
Robert Carissimi. Skunk Cabbage and Ferns at the White Memorial Foundation, Litchfield, Connecticut. 1985

Some concentrate on political work. Some emphasize hikes, birdwatching, and botanizing. Some fill other needs: the Dallas group is the largest singles organization in that city, for instance, and there are Sierra Singles groups in many cities.

All the chapters conduct outings, an estimated eight thousand a year total. There are committees on everything from Native American sites to the environmental effects of nuclear war. The San Francisco Bay Chapter, after several years of wrangling, established a gay and lesbian Sierrans section. If there is no group or section of the Sierra Club that conducts the kind of activities members want, they are encouraged to invent one.

As the Sierra Club celebrates its centennial, the environmental movement is growing, both in numbers of supporters and in breadth of agenda. With old and new groups of its own, the Club addresses concerns as local as a city park and as international as global warming and ozone depletion. All volunteers are welcome, all are needed. With its unique blend of volunteer control over a highly skilled professional staff, backed up by hundreds of thousands of deeply committed members, the Sierra Club forges ahead to carry out the vision John Muir held when he helped found the organization one hundred years ago: "To do something for wildness and make the mountains glad."

Philip Hyde. Dunes at Granite Creek,
Grand Canyon National Park, Arizona.
1956

Willard Clay. Sunset on the Oregon
Coast, Bandon State Park. 1987

David Muench. Bunch Grass in the San
Luis Valley, Sangre de Cristo Range,
Sierra Blanca, Colorado. 1972

Kathleen Norris Cook. Moonrise over Blue Mesa, Painted Desert, Arizona. 1981

Tom Algire. Cholla and Tamarisk,
Canyon de Chelly, Arizona. 1983

ABOVE RIGHT
Willard Clay. Mixed Flower Scene on
the Forest Floor in the Mosquito Range,
San Isabel National Forest, Colorado.
1986

OPPOSITE
Jeff Gnass. Maroon Creek Canyon,
White River National Forest, Colorado.
1982

Carr Clifton. Giraud Peak, Dusy Basin,
Kings Canyon National Park,
California. 1985

NOTES

1 Muir, *The Story of My Boyhood and Youth*, 1.

2 See especially Fox, *John Muir and His Legacy*, and Turner, *Rediscovering America*.

3 Muir, *The Yosemite*, 2.

4 "Yosemite, the Story of an Idea," *Sierra Club Bulletin*, 33, no. 3 (March 1948): 47.

5 This is not meant in any way to detract from Yellowstone, whose geothermal wonders are surrounded by two million acres of glorious wilderness. For political purposes, however, past, present, and future, it is important to take the side of Yosemite, as the Sierra Club has done for most of a century.

6 The federal government and some state governments mounted survey expeditions to map the uncharted territories under their jurisdiction. Thus, John Wesley Powell's U.S. Geological Survey explored and mapped the Colorado Plateau; Whitney's California Geological Survey mapped the Sierra Nevada.

7 Tilden, *The National Parks*, 306.

8 An organizational meeting was held a week before, on May 28; that date is often cited as the birthday of the organization.

9 Powell, *Report on the Lands*, 8.

10 *Sierra Club Bulletin* 3, no. 1 (1895).

11 Muir, *The Yosemite*, 197, in the 1988 ed.

12 Jones, *John Muir and the Sierra Club: The Battle for Yosemite*, 168.

13 Whether Pinchot was altogether proud of his achievement in later years is open to some question: Neither Hetch Hetchy nor the Sierra Club merits a single mention in his 522-page autobiography.

14 *Sierra Club Bulletin* 10, no. 1, 1916.

15 *Sierra Club Bulletin*, 17, no. 1 (February 1932): 1.

16 *Ibid.*, 19, no. 3 (June 1934): 99.

17 Detailed and engaging accounts of the first ascent of Shiprock, along with forty-nine other notable climbs, are contained in Roper and Steck, *Fifty Classic Climbs*.

18 Brower, *For Earth's Sake: The Life and Times of David Brower*, 187.

19 Cohen, *The History of the Sierra Club 1892–1970*, 46.

20 Quoted in Gilliam, *Voices for the Earth*, 186.

21 David Brower, ed., *The Meaning of Wilderness to Science* (San Francisco: Sierra Club Books, 1960), v.

22 Following his exploration of the Colorado River starting in 1869, Powell recommended establishment of the Bureau of Reclamation, primarily to irrigate the arid lands of the West.

23 *The Exploration of the Colorado River and Its Canyons* (New York: Dover Publications, 1961), 232.

24 Eliot Porter, *The Place No One Knew: Glen Canyon on the Colorado* (San Francisco: Sierra Club Books, 1963), vii.

25 Adams and Newhall, *This Is the American Earth*, xiv.

26 Muir, *Travels in Alaska*, 125.

OPPOSITE
Robert Carissimi. Stream, White Mountain National Forest, New Hampshire. 1987

CHRONOLOGY
OF THE
SIERRA CLUB

1892 Sierra Club incorporated on June 4 with 182 charter members. John Muir elected first president. In its first conservation campaign, Club leads effort to defeat a proposed reduction in the boundaries of Yosemite National Park, California.

1893 The first *Sierra Club Bulletin*, forerunner of *Sierra* magazine, is issued. President Benjamin Harrison establishes a thirteen million-acre Sierra Forest Reserve in California. Club establishes an office in the California Academy of Sciences building in San Francisco.

1894 Sierra Club climbers place registers on the summits of six California peaks and begin recording ascents.

1895 John Muir and professors Joseph LeConte and William Dudley speak on preserving national parks and forest reserves at the Club's annual meeting in San Francisco. Muir urges the return of Yosemite Valley to federal management.

1896 Club publishes a map of Yosemite Valley and the central Sierra Nevada.

1897 Club urges strengthening of public forest policy and supports U.S. Forestry Commission recommendations for additional "national forest parks," including Grand Canyon and Mount Rainier. Membership reaches 350.

1898 Club establishes office in Yosemite Valley to aid and educate visitors; William Colby is attendant. Club urges establishment of parks to preserve coast redwoods in California.

1899 Congress establishes Mount Rainier National Park through legislation based on a statement prepared by the Sierra Club and several other organizations.

1900 Club assists in preserving the North Grove of Calaveras Big Trees, east of Stockton, California.

1901 In the Club's first outing, William Colby leads ninety-six participants on a trip to Yosemite Valley and Tuolumne Meadows, beginning a tradition of annual High Trips.

1902 Sierra Club High Trip visits Kings Canyon, south of Yosemite.

1903 President Theodore Roosevelt visits Yosemite with John Muir. High Trip to Kern Canyon includes an ascent of Mount Whitney by 139 Club members.

LeConte Memorial Lodge built in Yosemite Valley in memory of charter member Joseph LeConte, Sr. Club office moves to Mills Building in San Francisco. Membership reaches 663.

1904 Club's first local outings begin in San Francisco area.

1905 In one of the Club's first conservation victories, the California legislature agrees to return Yosemite Valley to federal management. Fifty-six members on the annual High Trip climb Mount Rainier in the first Club outing outside of California.

1906 San Francisco earthquake destroys Club records and library.

1907 Club submits a resolution to the Secretary of the Interior opposing damming of Hetch Hetchy Valley, north of Yosemite.

1908 Club membership reaches 1,000.

1909 Club sponsors trail construction to make the High Sierra above Kings Canyon accessible.

1910 Club advocates establishment of Glacier National Park in Montana. Devil's Postpile and Rainbow Falls in California are endangered by a proposed reservoir. Poll of members shows that the majority support Club's position on Hetch Hetchy.

1911 Devil's Postpile National Monument established, largely through the work of Club member Walter Huber. Activists organize Club chapter in Southern California which later becomes the Angeles Chapter.

1912 Club urges establishment of a National Park Service and buys inholding at Soda Springs in Yosemite National Park.

1913 Congress allows flooding of Hetch Hetchy Valley. Southern California Chapter builds Muir Lodge near Los Angeles.

1914 Last Sierra Club outing to Hetch Hetchy Valley. John Muir dies on December 24.

1915 Club wins passage of California legislation appropriating $10,000 for construction of the John Muir Trail, the first of five such appropriations. Joseph LeConte, Jr., becomes Club's second president.

1916 Club supports bill establishing the National Park Service. Club member Stephen Mather is appointed National Park Service director.

1917 Club protests grazing in national parks as an unnecessary wartime measure.

1918 Club urges enlargement of California's Sequoia National Park to include headwaters of Kings and Kern rivers. About 140 members serve in World War I.

1919 Ansel Adams becomes custodian of LeConte Lodge in Yosemite Valley. Club supports formation of Save-the-Redwoods League.

1920 Club opposes plan to build dams in Yellowstone National Park in Wyoming, Montana, and Idaho.

1921 Club urges purchase of redwoods in California's Humboldt County for a state park.

1922 Mount Shasta Alpine Lodge is built by Club members in California.

1923 Federal Power Commission rules against proposals to build hydroelectric dams on the Kings River in the Sierra Nevada, in part due to effective Club protests. Club helps National Park Service purchase Redwood Meadow for inclusion in Sequoia National Park enlargement.

1924 Club advocates establishment of a California State Park Commission and a statewide survey of land suitable for state parks. San Francisco Bay Chapter organized.

1925 Club inaugurates a photographic collection for loan to educational and other institutions.

1926 Congress adds Kern and Kaweah regions, including Mount Whitney, to Sequoia National Park.

1927 California legislature establishes a State Park Commission, with Sierra Club Secretary William Colby as its first chairman. Aurelia Harwood becomes Club president, the first woman to serve in that position.

1928 Club contributes $1,000 toward purchase and donation to the National Park Service of a private inholding in Sequoia National Park.

1929 Club works with San Francisco Bay Area conservationists to win establishment of Mount Tamalpais State Park.

1930 Membership reaches 2,537.

1931 On annual High Trip, Club members Francis Farquhar and Robert Underhill introduce the use of rope and belaying techniques in rock climbing. They later lead first ascents of routes on the North Palisade, Thunderbolt Peak, and the east face of Mount Whitney, California.

1932 Club urges National Park Service to investigate Alaska's Admiralty Island as a national park. Winter Sports Committee organized. Club moves office to Mills Tower in San Francisco.

1933 Muir Lodge destroyed by flood. Club advises Park Service on rebuilding Tioga Road in Yosemite National Park.

1934 Club builds Clair Tappaan Lodge near Donner Pass in the Sierra and publishes *A Guide to the John Muir Trail*, by Walter Starr.

1935 Legislation introduced to establish Kings Canyon National Park; Club opposes a proposed road into the area. Club supports legislation to create Olympic National Park in Washington and urges that the boundaries of Death Valley National Monument be extended to include a portion of the Panamint Range, California.

1936 Ansel Adams travels with his photographs to Washington, D.C., to lobby the Roosevelt administration to preserve Kings Canyon and the surrounding High Sierra.

1937 Club opposes construction of a tunnel to divert water under Rocky Mountain National Park.

1938 Club protests proposal to dam Yellowstone Lake. John Muir Trail completed, and Club conducts first burro and knapsack outings. Club Directors meet with Interior Secretary Harold Ickes to support establishment of Kings Canyon as a wilderness national park.

1939 Club produces its first film, *Sky-Land Trails of the Kings*, and publishes a booklet to promote establishment of Kings Canyon National Park. Club party climbs Shiprock in New Mexico.

1940 Congress establishes Kings Canyon National Park. First Club base camp outing.

1941 Club helps enlarge Anza State Park in the California desert. Club film, *Skis to the Sky-Land*, encourages ski mountaineering.

1942 Club contributes $2,500 toward Park Service acquisition of privately owned property on Tenaya Lake in Yosemite National Park.

1943 Club successfully defends Jackson Hole National Monument in Wyoming and opposes repeal of the Antiquities Act which allows establishment of national monuments. Outings are temporarily discontinued due to war.

1944 Club seeks to protect sequoia trees in the South Calaveras Grove.

1945 More than 1,000 Club members serve in the armed forces in World War II.

1946 Club supports legislation to establish Joshua Tree National Monument, California. Club purchases Flora and Azalea lakes to protect one of the last natural areas near California's Donner Pass.

1947 Club succeeds in campaign to preserve San Gorgonio Primitive Area and works to protect Olympic National Park and Jackson Hole National Monument. Club publishes first edition of *The Sierra Club: A Handbook*.

1948 Club opposes construction of Glacier View Dam which would flood 20,000 acres of Glacier National Park. Club successfully protests hydroelectric dams proposed for Kings Canyon National Park.

1949 Secretaries of Interior and Army reject Glacier View Dam after a public hearing in which the Club is represented by the great biologist and explorer Olaus Murie. Club campaigns to preserve South Calaveras Grove and Butano Forest. At the suggestion of Director Norman Livermore, Club sponsors a High Sierra Wilderness Conference, predecessor of fourteen biennial wilderness conferences.

1950 Interior Secretary orders study of alternatives to damming Oregon's Rogue River. After a long battle by the Club, Congress enlarges Grand Teton National Park to include Jackson Hole National Monument. Atlantic Chapter, comprising eighteen eastern states and the District of Columbia, becomes first Club chapter outside of California.

1951 In a campaign viewed as a test of the integrity of national parks and a major challenge for the Sierra Club, Club decides to fight to protect Dinosaur National Monument, Utah, from two dams proposed by the federal government. A special edition of the *Sierra Club Bulletin* covers the issue for members. At the Second Biennial Wilderness Conference, Howard Zahniser introduces the idea of legislative protection for wilderness areas.

1952 Interior Secretary Oscar Chapman temporarily protects Dinosaur National Monument by ordering a study of alternative dam sites. David Brower becomes the Club's first executive director. Club protests as Los Angeles renews applications to build dams in Kings Canyon National Park.

1953 Some two hundred Club members take six-day raft trips down the Yampa and Green rivers in Dinosaur National Monument. Club produces *Wilderness River Trail* to promote Dinosaur's values. President Harry Truman adds 47,000 acres to Olympic National Park.

1954 Secretary of the Interior Douglas McKay renews plan to build dams in Dinosaur National Monument; Club continues battle to save the park. River touring committee established. Club publishes *Climber's Guide to the High Sierra*.

1955 Dinosaur controversy continues, as do Club efforts to publicize it. Alfred Knopf publishes *This Is Dinosaur*, edited by Wallace Stegner, while the Club film *Two Yosemites* compares the damming of Hetch Hetchy to plans to dam Dinosaur.

1956 Federal water developers drop plans to dam Dinosaur National Monument, but begin construction of Glen Canyon Dam. Club supports establishment of national wilderness system proposed by Senator Hubert Humphrey and Representative John Saylor. Club leads first outings to Washington's North Cascades. Sierra Club Council created. Membership reaches 10,000.

1957 Club sponsors Fifth Biennial Wilderness Conference on "Wildlands in Our Civilization." *Wilderness Alps of Stehekin* is filmed to publicize the North Cascades, Washington.

1958 Outing Committee organizes the first service trips in which hikers work on trail maintenance and back-country management projects. Club fails to prevent reconstruction of Tioga Road through Yosemite's Tenaya Lake area.

1959 Sixth Wilderness Conference focuses on "The Meaning of Wilderness to Science." Participants raise the issue of the environmental effects of world overpopulation.

1960 The Sierra Club Foundation established. Club's Exhibit Format book series launched with publication of *This Is the American Earth* by Ansel Adams and Nancy Newhall. Club urges Forest Service to adopt a comprehensive system of land-use classifications and to hold public hearings on plans that would alter the wilderness character of national forest lands. Membership reaches 16,000.

1961 Seventh Wilderness Conference discusses "The American Heritage of Wilderness," emphasizing the role of wilderness in molding the American character. Club opposes Project Chariot, a plan to use nuclear explosives to excavate a harbor in Alaska. Michael McCloskey hired as the Club's first field representative, serving the Northwest. William Colby is first recipient of the Club's John Muir Award.

1962 Congress establishes Point Reyes and Padre Island national seashores to preserve endangered coastlines in California and Texas. Club publishes Eliot Porter's "*In Wildness Is the Preservation of the World*," the first color volume in the Exhibit Format Series.

1963 Club launches campaign to protect the Grand Canyon following congressional proposals to dam and flood parts of it. Club Directors endorse proposal to seek a North Cascades National Park. Club opens Washington, D.C., office.

1964 After years of battle, Congress passes the Wilderness Act, the first wilderness protection legislation in the world. Congress also creates the Land and Water Conservation Fund and provides for review of public land laws. Club advocates establishment of Redwood National Park and asks California Governor Pat Brown to complete acquisition of state redwood parks.

1965 Club continues campaign to keep dams out of the Grand Canyon. Congress begins consideration of legislation to establish Redwood National Park. William Colby Memorial Library opens. Membership reaches 33,000.

1966 Club's full-page newspaper ads urging protection of the Grand Canyon prompt Internal Revenue Service to rule that donations to the Club are no longer tax-deductible. Ruling stimulates an outpouring of contributions. Redwood and North Cascades campaigns continue. Conservation Department established with Michael McCloskey as director. Patrick Goldsworthy receives Club's first William Colby Award.

1967 Club celebrates 75th anniversary. Led by Club President Edgar Wayburn, Club directors urge protection of natural areas in Alaska. First of the highly successful series of Sierra Club calendars published.

1968 Club succeeds in campaigns to stop dams in the Grand Canyon and to establish Redwood National Park. Congress enacts a Wild and Scenic Rivers System. San Rafael Wilderness in California becomes the first new area designated after passage of the Wilderness Act. Hike-in at Mineral King protests plan to develop a massive ski resort in the area. Club leads successful fight to expand the Land and Water Conservation Fund. Congress establishes North Cascades National Park, rewarding a long campaign in which Club played a key role.

1969 Club wins suit to stop pollution in Lake Superior and joins a coalition of environmental groups opposing development of a jetport in Florida's Everglades. Michael McCloskey becomes Club's second Executive Director. Conservation Department begins publication of the *National News Report.*

1970 Congress enacts the National Environmental Policy Act, establishes the Environmental Protection Agency, and denies funds for Everglades jetport. Club leads a coalition that defeats the National Timber Supply Act which threatened old growth in the national forests. Membership passes 114,000, and Club chapters cover all fifty states.

1971 In a victory for a coalition that included the Club, Congress defeats funding for the supersonic transport (SST). Alaska Native Claims Settlement Act passes, granting the Secretary of Interior authority to set aside up to 80 million acres in national-interest lands. Club proposals prompt Forest Service to inventory roadless areas in national forests. Club's International Program begins operation. Inner City Outings program established. Sierra Club Legal Defense Fund founded.

1972 Club leads defeat of legislation that would overhaul public land laws to favor commodity interests. Congress authorizes a system of marine sanctuaries and designates the Golden Gate and Gateway East national recreation areas. Water Pollution Control Act passes over President Richard Nixon's veto. Club lawsuit leads to a ban on domestic use of DDT. Club leads campaign that convinces Interior Secretary Rogers Morton to set aside 83.4 million acres of national-interest lands in Alaska. Western Canada becomes first Club chapter outside U.S. Club representatives attend first Conference on the Human Environment in Stockholm, Sweden.

1973 Club launches campaign to defend the Clean Air Act against auto industry opposition. After years of effort, the Highway Trust Fund is opened to permit funding of mass transit. A lawsuit by Club and other conservationists spurs a court to declare clear-cutting illegal in national forests in West Virginia. Club pushes Congress to pass the Ports and Waterways Safety Act following a massive oil spill in San Francisco Bay.

1974 Club successfully lobbies to establish Big Thicket Preserve in Texas and Big Cypress Preserve in Florida. Congress passes wilderness legislation for several eastern states, protecting 250,000 acres. Army Corps of Engineers abandons plan for a forty-four-mile levee at the confluence of the Mississippi and Missouri rivers.

1975 With Club support, Congress passes legislation promoting energy conservation. Hells Canyon National Recreation Area established. Club lawsuit broadens applicability of the National Environmental Policy Act to U.S. actions having marine and international impacts. Club sponsors International Earthcare Conference in New York. Club wins long-sought additions to Grand Canyon National Park and blocks transfer of several national wildlife ranges from the Fish and Wildlife Service to other agencies. Club headquarters moves to 530 Bush Street in San Francisco.

1976 Club wins campaign to repeal obsolete land disposal policies and establish a wilderness review program for the Bureau of Land Management's 341 million acres. Club promotes passage of the National Forest Management Act, which offers greater protection for national forests. Club lawsuits temporarily preserve parts of Admiralty Island in Alaska and block the proposed Kaiparowitz Powerplant in Utah. Club supports passage of the reform Coal Leasing Act and establishment of a 303,508-acre Alpine Lakes Wilderness in Washington. Sierra Club Committee on Political Education (SCCOPE) formed.

1977 Club joins successful effort to strengthen the Clean Air Act. Club leads a coalition to preserve Alaska's national-interest lands and persuades President Jimmy Carter to support a natural gas pipeline route that avoids the Arctic National Wildlife Range. Campaign to control strip mining abuses culminates in passage of the Surface Mining Control and Reclamation Act.

1978 Club wins a 48,000-acre addition to Redwood National Park, protecting the watershed of the earth's tallest trees. Congress passes Representative Phillip Burton's Omnibus Parks Bill which includes Santa Monica Mountains National Recreation Area, Pinelands National Reserve, eight wild and scenic rivers, and the addition of Mineral King to Sequoia National Park. Club works for passage of the Endangered American Wilderness Act which preserves 1.3 million acres. Club supports reform of offshore oil and gas leasing laws.

1979 Following the nuclear accident at Three Mile Island, Club calls for phased closure of all commercial reactors. Club activists work to improve wilderness proposals made in Forest Service study of roadless areas in national forests. Club cosponsors City Care Conference on the urban environment with the National Urban League. Club helps develop National Forest Management Act regulations for forest planning.

1980 Congress passes Alaska National Interest Lands Conservation Act designating 104 million acres of parks, wildlife refuges, and wilderness areas. Congress also preserves more than four million acres of wilderness in the lower forty-eight states. Club supports successful "Superfund" legislation to clean up toxic waste dumps and helps defeat a proposed Energy Mobilization Board which would have allowed waiver of environmental laws. SCCOPE brings Club into electoral campaigns for the first time.

1981 Sierra Club and other conservation groups gather more than one million petition signatures urging the ouster of Interior Secretary James Watt. Conservationists and local citizens join forces to prevent deployment of the MX missile in the Great Basin in Utah and Nevada. Club helps block oil and gas leasing off the California coast. Membership passes 200,000.

1982 Club helps block effort to weaken the Clean Air Act. SCCOPE activities expand. Environmentalists push Congress to stop Reagan administration from selling public lands and allowing energy exploration and development in wilderness areas. Club members involved in more than 170 congressional races and 150 state and local contests; Club-backed candidates win eighty percent of the races. Membership reaches 325,000.

1983 Club holds its first International Assembly in Snowmass, Colorado. Galveston Superport lawsuit reaffirms that environmental impact statements must consider all potential adverse effects. Another lawsuit compels the Forest Service to comply with state regulation of aerial herbicide spraying. A court responds to Club and Native American concerns and prevents road construction through proposed Siskiyou Wilderness in California. Following a decade of effort by the Club, Congress terminates funding for the Clinch River Breeder Reactor. James Watt resigns as Interior Secretary.

1984 Congress passes wilderness bills that protect 6.8 million acres in national forests and 1.4 million acres in national parks. Congress reauthorizes the Resource Conservation and Recovery Act requiring safety in the manufacture, storage, transportation, and disposal of toxic materials. Club wins lawsuit requiring EPA to regulate release of radioactive pollutants. Other lawsuits uphold Wild and Scenic River designation for five California rivers and protect provisions of a California farmland protection program.

1985 Club successfully supports reauthorization of strengthened Superfund law and Clean Water Act. Congress passes farm legislation with measures to protect wetlands and highly erodible land. Congress axes funding for the environmentally destructive Synthetic Fuels Corporation. Congress establishes the Clifty Wilderness in Kentucky and enlarges several wilderness areas in Texas. Douglas Wheeler appointed Executive Director; Michael McCloskey becomes Club Chairman. Club moves headquarters to 730 Polk Street in San Francisco.

1986 Club helps win congressional designation of 270,000-acre Columbia Gorge National Scenic Area, Washington, and supports enactment of a 76,000-acre Great Basin National Park in Nevada. Congress passes wilderness legislation for national forest areas in Georgia, Nebraska, and Tennessee. Water resources funding bill passes Congress with reforms sought by environmentalists. Legislation introduced to designate wilderness and national parks in the California desert.

1987 Congress passes reauthorization and expansion of the Clean Water Act over veto by President Reagan and designates wilderness areas in Michigan and Virginia. In a move opposed by the Club, EPA extends air pollution compliance deadlines for some urban areas by as much as twenty-five years. Joint Canada-U.S. Great Lakes water quality agreement expanded to address the impacts of toxic air pollution. Merced, Kings, and Kern rivers in Sierra Nevada win Wild and Scenic River protection. Forest Service agrees to protect 112 eastern rivers pending congressional action. Interior Secretary Donald Hodel proposes draining Hetch Hetchy Reservoir. Michael Fischer appointed Executive Director.

1988 Club awards "Clean Air" medals to 270 congressional representatives for their efforts on behalf of clean air legislation. As Congress continues work on clean air, EPA releases a study showing that 135 million Americans live in communities that fail to meet air pollution standards. NASA official tells Congress that the "greenhouse effect" is influencing global climate. Congress reauthorizes the Endangered Species Act, adds parts of forty rivers in Oregon to the National Wild and Scenic River System, and designates new wilderness areas in Alabama, Montana, Oklahoma, and Washington. Club celebrates John Muir's 150th birthday.

1989 Club runs full-page ad in *The New York Times* condemning North America's largest oil spill, in Prince William Sound, Alaska. Under pressure from the Sierra Club and other groups, the World Bank withdraws a $500 million loan to Brazil that would have led to construction of 147 new dams and inundation of large areas of the Amazon. Spotted owl listed by the federal government as a threatened species, highlighting the plight of the remaining ancient forests of the Pacific Northwest. Forest wilderness bill for Nevada signed into law, protecting some 733,000 acres. Nomination of James Cason as Assistant Secretary of Agriculture withdrawn under pressure from environmental groups.

1990 Clean Air Act reauthorization passed, with Sierra Club leading the grassroots effort. Improves protection against acid rain, toxic air pollutants, and urban air pollution. Arizona Wilderness Act signed into law; it protects 1.1 million acres of BLM land and 1.3 million acres of wildlife refuge lands. Petroglyphs Park, comprising 7,370 acres, established near Albuquerque to protect some 17,000 petroglyphs. Legislation enacted increasing protection for the Tongass National Forest of southeastern Alaska. In the wake of the *Exxon Valdez* accident, Congress enacts new oil spill liability and compensation law. 1990 Farm Bill increases protection for wetlands. Congress passes a bill that establishes U.S. policy for protecting the environment of Antarctica. Strengthened Coastal Zone Management act signed into law.

1991 Club's "Celebrate Wild Alaska" event in Washington, D.C., kicks off campaign to protect coastal plain of Arctic Wildlife Refuge. Club launches program to enhance lobbying at the state or provincial level throughout North America. Club launches the Centennial Celebration—the beginning of its 100th year.

Chronology adapted from The Sierra Club: A Guide *(San Francisco, 1989).*

CREDITS

For their generous assistance in obtaining the illustrations, the editors thank Joanne Hurley, Phoebe Adams, and Helmi Nock of the Sierra Club staff for their considerable guidance and attention, as well as Club leaders Michael McCloskey, Edgar Wayburn, Richard M. Leonard, and David Brower. Thanks are also due to Steve Griffiths of the Outings Department, Jonathan King and Alex Woodruff of *Sierra*, Jon Beckmann and Sam Petersen of Sierra Club Books, and Anna Rodriques and Barbara Lekisch. Appreciation goes to Larry Dineen, Richard Ogar, Mary Morganti, Dan Johnston, Lauren Lassleben, and Bonnie Hardwick of the Bancroft Library staff, University of California, Berkeley; William Turnage and Pamela Feld of the Ansel Adams Publishing Rights Trust; Therese Heyman, Darcy Coates, and Drew Johnson of the Oakland Museum; Nick Mills for access to the Robbins collection of Herbert W. Gleason photographs; and Linda Eade and Bob Woolard of the Yosemite National Park Research Library.

Following is a list of the copyrights © held by the color photographers whose work is illustrated in this book: Tom Algire; Christine Alicino; Morley Baer; Robert L. Carissimi; Mark Citret; Willard Clay; Carr Clifton; Kathleen Norris Cook; David C. Fritts; Gustavo Gilabert/J.B. Pictures; Jeff Gnass; Philip Hyde; Robert Glenn Ketchum, 1991; Warren Marr; David Muench, 1990; B. Nation/Sygma; Eliot Porter Archives, Amon Carter Museum, Fort Worth, Texas; Galen Rowell; Ted Schiffman/Peter Arnold, Inc.; Larry Ulrich; John Ward; and Art Wolfe.

BIBLIOGRAPHY

꙾

Adams, Ansel, and Nancy Newhall. *This Is the American Earth*. San Francisco: Sierra Club, 1960.

Brower, David R. *For Earth's Sake: The Life and Times of David Brower*. Layton, Utah: Gibbs Smith Publisher, 1990.

_____, ed. *The Sierra Club Manual of Ski Mountaineering*. Berkeley: University of California Press, 1942; San Francisco: Sierra Club, 1962.

_____, ed. *The Sierra Club Wilderness Handbook*. San Francisco: Sierra Club, 1951.

_____. *Work in Progress*. Layton, Utah: Gibbs Smith Publisher, 1991.

Bryan, C. D. B. *The National Geographic Society: 100 Years of Adventure and Discovery*. New York: Harry N. Abrams, Inc., 1987.

Carr, Patrick, ed. *The Sierra Club: A Guide*. San Francisco: Sierra Club Books, 1989.

Clyde, Norman. *Norman Clyde of the High Sierra: Rambles through the Range of Light*. San Francisco: Scrimshaw Press, 1971.

Cohen, Michael P. *The History of the Sierra Club 1892–1970*. San Francisco: Sierra Club Books, 1988.

Douglas, William O. *Muir of the Mountains*. Boston: North Star Books, 1961.

Engberg, Robert, and Donald Wesling, eds. *John Muir — to Yosemite and Beyond: Writings from the Years 1863 to 1875*. Madison, Wisc.: University of Wisconsin Press, 1980.

Farquhar, Francis P. *History of the Sierra Nevada*. Berkeley: University of California Press, 1965.

_____. *Place Names of the High Sierra*. San Francisco: Sierra Club, 1926.

Fox, Stephen. *John Muir and His Legacy: The American Conservation Movement*. Boston: Little, Brown, 1981.

Gilliam, Ann, ed. *Voices for the Earth: A Treasury of the Sierra Club Bulletin, 1893–1977*. San Francisco: Sierra Club Books, 1979.

Gilliam, Harold. *Island in Time: The Point Reyes Peninsula*. San Francisco, Sierra Club, 1962.

Jones, Holway R. *John Muir and the Sierra Club: The Battle for Yosemite*. San Francisco: Sierra Club, 1965.

Kimball, H. Stewart. *History of the Sierra Club Outing Committee, 1901–1972*. San Francisco: Sierra Club Outing Committee, 1990.

LeConte, Joseph. *A Journal of Ramblings through the High Sierras by the University "Excursion Party."* San Francisco: Sierra Club, 1924.

Leydet, François. *Time and the River Flowing, Grand Canyon*. San Francisco: Sierra Club, 1964.

McArdle, Phil, ed. *Exactly Opposite the Golden Gate: Essays on Berkeley's History*. Berkeley: Berkeley Historical Society, 1986.

McPhee, John. *Encounters with the Archdruid*. New York: Farrar, Straus and Giroux, 1971.

Mitchell, John G., and Constance L. Stallings, eds. *Ecotactics: The Sierra Club Handbook for Environment Activists*. New York: Pocket Books, 1970.

Muir, John. *The Mountains of California*. New York: Century Company, 1894; San Francisco: Sierra Club Books, 1988.

_____. *My First Summer in the Sierra*. Boston: Houghton Mifflin Company, 1911; San Francisco: Sierra Club Books, 1988.

_____. *The Story of My Boyhood and Youth*. Boston: Houghton Mifflin Company, 1913; San Francisco: Sierra Club Books, 1988.

_____. *The Yosemite*. New York: Houghton Mifflin Company, 1914; San Francisco: Sierra Club Books, 1988.

Nash, Roderick, ed. *Grand Canyon of the Living Colorado*. San Francisco: Sierra Club Books, 1970.

Pinchot, Gifford. *Breaking New Ground*. New York: Harcourt, Brace, 1947; Washington, D.C.: Island Press, 1988.

Porter, Eliot. *Summer Island, Penobscot Country*. San Francisco: Sierra Club, 1966.

Porter, Eliot, and Henry David Thoreau. *"In Wildness Is the Preservation of the World."* San Francisco: Sierra Club, 1962.

David Muench. Bald Cypresses— Trussum Pond, Delaware. 1981

Powell, John Wesley. *Report on the Lands of the Arid Region of the United States, With a More Detailed Account of the Lands of Utah*, ed. Wallace Stegner. Cambridge, Mass.: Harvard University Press, 1962.

Reisner, Marc. *Cadillac Desert*. New York: Viking, 1986.

Roper, Steve, and Allen Steck, eds. *Fifty Classic Climbs of North America*. San Francisco: Sierra Club Books, 1979.

Runte, Alfred. *Yosemite, the Embattled Wilderness*. Lincoln, Neb.: University of Nebraska Press, 1990.

Starr, Walter A., Jr.: *Guide to the John Muir Trail and the High Sierra Region*. San Francisco: Sierra Club, 1934.

Tilden, Freeman. *The National Parks: What They Mean to You and Me*. New York: Alfred A. Knopf, 1951.

Turner, Frederick. *Rediscovering America—John Muir in His Time and Ours*. New York: Viking, 1985; San Francisco: Sierra Club Books, 1987.

Udall, Stewart L. *The Quiet Crisis and the Next Generation*. Layton, Utah: Gibbs Smith Publisher, 1989.

Wolfe, Linnie Marsh. *Son of the Wilderness: The Life of John Muir*. New York: Alfred A. Knopf, 1945; Madison, Wisc.: University of Wisconsin Press, 1978.

Wright, Cedric. *Words of the Earth*. San Francisco: Sierra Club, 1960.

INDEX